HANOI
Including Ha Long Bay

DANA FILEK-GIBSON

Contents

Hanoi

Look for ★ to find recommended sights, activities, dining, and lodging.

Highlights

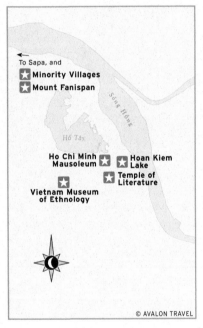

To Sapa, and
★ **Minority Villages**
★ **Mount Fanispan**

Sông Hồng

Hồ Tây

Ho Chi Minh Mausoleum ★   ★ **Hoan Kiem Lake**

★ **Temple of Literature**

★
Vietnam Museum of Ethnology

© AVALON TRAVEL

★ **Hoan Kiem Lake:** Take in the bustle and noise of downtown Hanoi from the shores of this legendary lake, where history and mythology meet (page 11).

★ **Ho Chi Minh Mausoleum:** Pay a visit to Vietnam's most revered national hero, embalmed and at peace under glass in a blocky, Soviet-style mausoleum (page 19).

★ **Temple of Literature:** A long series of lacquered pavilions and spacious courtyards, lotus ponds, and stone stelae, this Confucian temple marks the site of Vietnam's first university (page 22).

★ **Vietnam Museum of Ethnology:** Learn all there is to know about Vietnam's 54 ethnic groups, from the Kinh of the coast to the H'mong, Thai, Gia Rai, and scores of other lesser-known minorities that populate the country's mountainous interior (page 24).

★ **Minority Villages:** Whether perched on the steep cliffs of the Hoang Lien mountain range or sheltered by lush green river valleys, Sapa's minority villages are a world apart from the rest of the country (page 64).

★ **Mount Fansipan:** Reach the "Roof of Indochina" via a long, action-packed ascent that winds through clouds and over limestone ridges to the summit of Vietnam's highest peak (page 68).

I n a thousand-year-old city, you would expect some things to get lost in the mix, obscured by cramped shops and narrow houses or buried under the incessant blare of traffic. But along the busy streets of Hanoi, every era of the city's history

shines, in its gracefully aging cathedral, sturdy Communist architecture, and the vibrant Old Quarter. Whether you're wandering the bustling shopping streets of its older neighborhoods, diving into history at the Temple of Literature, or visiting the embalmed remains of Ho Chi Minh, Vietnam's most respected national hero, there's no denying that the soul of Vietnam lies in Hanoi.

The capital is sleek and sophisticated, playing the wise older sibling to Ho Chi Minh City's freewheeling antics down south. A well-established art scene and strong café culture permeate most of the city, along with a self-assuredness that comes from having survived a millennium of ups and downs. Flashy boutiques and shopping malls are beginning to make an appearance around town, a stark contrast to the narrow, teetering tube houses of the city's downtown districts.

Most travelers to Vietnam pass through the capital, not only for its sights, sounds, and savory cuisine, but also for its status as a hub, connecting popular destinations like Sapa and Ha Long Bay with the rest of Vietnam.

Hanoi is a place to savor rather than sightsee. While its eclectic attractions make for a fascinating, patchwork history, the main draw of the capital is its infectious energy, which permeates every nook and cranny of Hanoi's jam-packed neighborhoods.

HISTORY

The fertile, low-lying Red River Delta has been inhabited since prehistoric times. Well before it became the capital of Vietnam, the region was used as an administrative and political center by the Chinese, who colonized Vietnam for a millennium-long stretch beginning in 208 BC. The city's official history began in AD 1010, when emperor Ly Thai To moved the capital from Hoa Lu north to a bend on the western bank of the Red River.

Previous: Sapa's remote minority villages; downtown Hanoi at rush hour. **Above:** incense urn at the Temple of Literature.

Hanoi

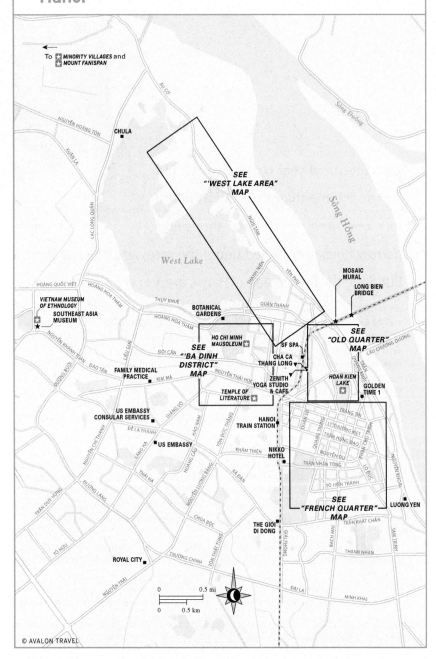

To ✚ MINORITY VILLAGES and
✦ MOUNT FANISPAN

CHULA

AU CO

NGUYỄN HOÀNG TÔN

XUÂN LA

LẠC LONG QUÂN

SEE
"WEST LAKE AREA"
MAP

Sông Đuống

Sông Hồng

West Lake

NGHI TÀM

THANH NIÊN

YÊN PHỤ

MOSAIC
MURAL

LONG BIEN
BRIDGE

HOÀNG QUỐC VIỆT

HOÀNG HOA THÁM

THUỴ KHUÊ

BOTANICAL
GARDENS

QUÁN THÁNH

VIETNAM MUSEUM
OF ETHNOLOGY

SOUTHEAST ASIA
MUSEUM

NGUYỄN KHÁNH TOÀN

HOÀNG HOA THÁM

ĐỘI CẤN

HO CHI MINH
MAUSOLEUM

SF SPA

SEE
"OLD QUARTER"
MAP

CẦU CHƯƠNG DƯƠNG

LẠC LONG QUÂN

LIỄU GIAI

ĐÀO TẤN

ĐƯỜNG BƯỞI

SEE
"BA DINH
DISTRICT"
MAP

NGUYỄN THÁI HỌC

CHA CA
THANG LONG

ZENITH
YOGA STUDIO
& CAFE

HOÀN KIẾM
LAKE

GOLDEN
TIME 1

FAMILY MEDICAL
PRACTICE

KIM MÃ

TEMPLE OF
LITERATURE

US EMBASSY
CONSULAR SERVICES

GIẢNG VÕ

ĐÊ LA THÀNH

HÀO NAM

TÔN ĐỨC THẮNG

HANOI
TRAIN STATION

TRÀNG THI

QUÁN SỨ

LÝ THƯỜNG KIỆT

TRẦN HƯNG ĐẠO

NGUYỄN DU

PHAN CHU TRINH

LÒ ĐÚC

NGUYỄN CHÍ THANH

US EMBASSY

LÁNG HẠ

HOÀNG CẦU

NGUYỄN LƯƠNG BẰNG

KHÂM THIÊN

NIKKO
HOTEL

TRẦN NHÂN TÔNG

TÔ HIẾN THÀNH

NGUYỄN KHOÁI

LƯƠNG YÊN

THÁI HÀ

XÃ ĐÀN

ĐƯỜNG LÁNG

TRẦN DUY HƯNG

TÔ HIỆU

CHÙA BỘC

TÔN THẤT TÙNG

THE GIỚI
DI ĐỘNG

GIẢI PHÓNG

SEE
"FRENCH QUARTER"
MAP

BẠCH MAI

TRẦN KHÁT CHÂN

TAM TRINH

ROYAL CITY

TRƯỜNG CHINH

THANH NHÀN

NGUYỄN TRÃI

ĐẠI LA

MINH KHAI

0   0.5 mi
0   0.5 km

© AVALON TRAVEL

Originally known as Thang Long ("ascending dragon"), the imperial citadel remained in this spot for centuries.

At the turn of the 19th century, emperor Gia Long, the first of the Nguyen Dynasty, moved his capital to Hue, situated at the center of the country. During much of the Nguyen Dynasty's reign, Hanoi served as a regional capital. It received its current moniker in 1831, courtesy of emperor Minh Mang, Gia Long's son and successor. The city later reclaimed its capital status in 1902, when the colonial French government chose it as the head of French Indochina. It continued to serve as the seat of power after Ho Chi Minh declared Vietnamese independence in 1945. Nine years later, the Geneva Accords of 1954 granted northern Vietnam to the Viet Minh, who carried out their political operations in the grand colonial buildings left behind by the French.

The American War ushered in darker days, with heavy bombing reducing large parts of the city to rubble. Long Bien Bridge saw routine bombardments, while Bach Mai Hospital was almost completely destroyed during the Christmas bombings of 1972. The damage to the city would take years to rebuild. After the war, Hanoi struggled to regain its footing, through Vietnam's 1979 border war with China and the poor economic policies that followed reunification. When the country's *doi moi* reforms were enacted, allowing for greater economic freedom, Vietnam began to blossom into the country that it is today, bringing Hanoi out of its misery and back on the path to prosperity.

PLANNING YOUR TIME

Hanoi is no more than a three-day affair, thanks to its compact size, allowing visitors to cover plenty of ground in a short time. For additional adventures, such as Perfume Pagoda or Tam Coc, set aside an extra day. Trips to Sapa require as few as two days or as many as five, if you have time to spare.

Most museums are closed on Mondays, and many pagodas close for at least two hours for lunch. Sightsee in the mornings, when more of the city's attractions are open.

Weather conditions in Hanoi are different from the tropical temperatures of the lower half of the country. Between November and February, Hanoi gets cold, with a steady mist and temperatures 50-60°F. Conditions become more pleasant around March and stay that way until the end of May, when temperatures start to rise. The heat reaches unbearable, sweltering temps in August, before another brief period of mild weather in September and October.

ORIENTATION

Hanoi is divvied up into 12 districts, 17 communes, and one hamlet, though most travelers stick to the downtown districts and the areas just beyond.

Hoan Kiem District is home to the eponymous Hoan Kien Lake, Hanoi's most famous landmark and a useful point of reference when navigating the city. Hoan Kiem is comprised of the bustling Old Quarter, where much of the city's commercial activity takes place, the posh French Quarter, and, along its western side, the Cathedral District. Along with picturesque St. Joseph's Cathedral, the Cathedral District houses cheap backpacker accommodations and trendy boutiques.

Northwest of Hoan Kiem, Ba Dinh District is where many of the capital's 20th-century historical sights are situated.

North of these downtown districts, Tay Ho (West Lake) is more upscale, with a residential feel and plenty of high-end shops and restaurants.

Hanoi's streets are tricky to get the hang of, with windy and narrow streets, and street names that change several times over the course of a mile. There are plenty of English-speaking residents downtown who can help to point you in the right direction. The city's public bus system is well-organized, affordable, has wide coverage, and has frequent service downtown and in other tourist-driven areas. *Xe om* and taxis are abundant and businesses are well-marked with street addresses.

Old Quarter

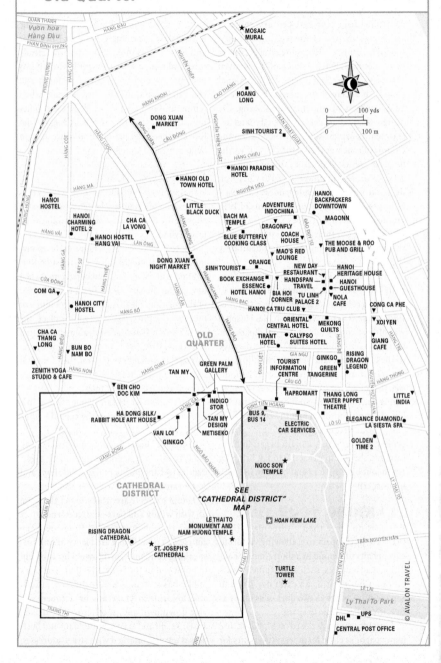

Sights

Hanoi's attractions span the entirety of its illustrious history, covering everything from imperial relics to colonial grandeur, the Communist revolution, and beyond. Scores of age-old pagodas dot the downtown neighborhoods, rubbing shoulders with crumbling art-deco architecture, a pair of legendary lakes, a few blocky Soviet-style buildings, and several museums that showcase the best of Hanoi's art, history, and culture.

This is the kind of place in which the journey rivals the destination. Rather than hop in a cab to the Temple of Literature, enlist the services of a cyclo driver or head for Ba Dinh district on foot. Even if it takes an extra hour and a few wrong turns, exploring the city this way brings its vibrancy to life.

OLD QUARTER

A teeming, tight-knit neighborhood barely contained by the tiny streets north of Hoan Kiem Lake, the historic Old Quarter is bright, chaotic, and fun. Hanoi's most visited commercial district, it has been in business for centuries and holds its own amid the recent crop of shopping malls and high-end stores that have sprung up elsewhere in town. Throngs of shoppers, street vendors, motorbikes, and storefronts crowd the narrow one-way streets and bustling alleys of this dense neighborhood, its cluster of skinny shops and tube houses acting as a large central market.

★ Hoan Kiem Lake

The focal point of the Old Quarter, Hoan Kiem Lake (corner of Dinh Tien Hoang and Le Thai To) is tranquility surrounded by chaos, its placid water ringed by traffic. Legend has it that emperor Le Thai To received a magical sword from the heavens, which he used to drive the Ming Chinese out of Vietnam in the early 15th century. After his victory, the king was rowing on the lake when a massive turtle appeared, took the sword from his belt, and sank back into the depths below. Le Thai To realized that the blade had been returned to its original owner, thus the lake became known as Hoan Kiem ("Lake of the Returned Sword"). On a small island near the southern end of the water is Turtle

Turtle Tower, Hoan Kiem Lake

A Long Weekend in Hanoi

While the thousand-year-old city holds plenty of history, the most captivating moment in Hanoi is the present. Follow this three-day itinerary to explore the storied past of the capital while experiencing the best of a modern-day Vietnamese metropolis at the same time. Taxis, *xe om,* and public buses are widely available, but it's recommended that you walk unless otherwise specified. Traveling by foot allows travelers to get the real feel of Hanoi's topsy-turvy energy.

DAY 1

Follow the locals and start your day early with breakfast at the hotel or a piping hot bowl of pho on the street. Any good Hanoian adventure begins with a trip to Hoan Kiem Lake, the epicenter of town, followed by nearby Ngoc Son Temple. From the northern edge of the water, you should be able to enlist the services of a cyclo driver, who will ferry you around the narrow, chaotic streets of the Old Quarter in order to witness the city in full swing. If you're up for it, walking is also an option, though the uninitiated will find downtown Hanoi's streets hectic. There are ample opportunities for shopping along Hang Gai and around the web of streets north of the lake.

Around lunchtime, you'll want to head toward St. Joseph's Cathedral on the western flank of the lake. Swing by the Le Thai To Monument and Nam Huong Temple, overlooking Hoan Kiem on the way, before cutting in toward the church. If you're feeling peckish, tuck into a savory bowl of *chao suon* (rice porridge), served daily in the alley near the cathedral, or visit the clutch of chic international restaurants sitting in the shadow of its towers. Nearby, Minh Thuy is another delicious and affordable option, while the Hanoi Social Club offers a tasty, unique alternative. Finish off your midday meal in true Vietnamese form at one of the cafés around St. Joseph's. Several cheap local street cafés offer plastic stools and affordable coffee and tea, while the cozy Hanoi House provides the same setting with a touch more ambience.

In the afternoon, make your way toward Hoa Lo Prison for a bit of history before turning east toward the top-notch Vietnamese Women's Museum. As the day winds down, stroll and shop along trendy Trang Tien street or pay a visit to the Opera House nearby. Enjoy a sunset drink from the terrace bar of the Press Club or grab a seat street-side in the artsy front room of Tadioto.

Dinner is left up to you, as you'll probably want to hop on a *xe om* or grab a cab to reach one of Hanoi's more authentic local meals. Ngon makes a great choice, as do the *cha ca* (pan-fried fish) restaurants a few blocks north of the lake. If you're up for some live entertainment in the evening, the band at Minh's Jazz Club puts on a nightly show, as do a rotating list of acts at Swing.

Tower, a structure built in 1886 to honor Le Thai Totower. During the French occupation, the tower held a small version of the Statue of Liberty, but it was destroyed when the city was wrested from French rule.

The lake and its surrounding park are a meeting place for locals. If you're lucky, you may spot the lake's sole remaining turtle, considered the offspring of the legendary one.

Ngoc Son Temple

On a small islet near the northern end of Hoan Kiem Lake, the grounds of Ngoc Son Temple (Dinh Tien Hoang, 7am-6pm summer, 7:30am-5pm winter, VND20,000, free for children under 15) originally served as a fishing dock for emperor Le Thanh Tong during the 15th century. Though the structure you see wasn't built until 1865, this small patch of land once housed a palace and, later, a pagoda. Ngoc Son Temple combines its Buddhist past with Confucian and Taoist influences.

The temple's front half is dedicated to Quan Cong, a loyal and courageous Chinese general of the Shu Han Dynasty. A flurry of red, black, and gold lacquerwork encircles his three-tiered altar, laden with fruit offerings. Alongside Quan Cong's beloved red horse is La To, a practitioner of traditional medicine and Taoist spirit.

DAY 2

You'll want to get an early jump on your second day, as the sights west of Hoan Kiem Lake require time and patience. In the morning, hop on a bus from the northern edge of the lake to Ba Dinh Square, where you can queue up for a visit to Ho Chi Minh Mausoleum. Dress respectfully; the rules are strict here. After you've made your way through the procession, you can snap photos of the square or head back toward Uncle Ho's famous stilt house and the One Pillar Pagoda. From here, those interested in learning more about Vietnam's war-related history should chart a course for the Military History Museum, while travelers who'd rather explore a local neighborhood can wander down the maze of alleys that precede B-52 Lake. This trip allows you to get a closer look at life in the capital.

Around noon, head south toward the Temple of Literature. Just across the street, KOTO is a busy lunchtime destination and great spot for a meal. Once you've paid a visit to the temple, you can wander back to the Old Quarter along Nguyen Thai Hoc, shopping as you go, or spend an hour at the Museum of Fine Arts nearby. Take the rest of the afternoon to relax and then set off again in the early evening for any one of Hanoi's local *bia hoi* (freshly brewed light beer) shops. The area around *bia hoi corner* in the Old Quarter offers a host of affordable street-side dining options as well as a collection of lively dance floors and laid-back hangouts.

DAY 3

Spend the morning at the Museum of Ethnology west of downtown. Because it's a trek and the museum itself is extensive, you'll want to allow ample time to explore the grounds, which include several outdoor replicas of traditional minority houses. Head back toward West Lake around noon for a roadside bowl of *bun cha* (grilled meat and rice noodles in fish sauce) on Hang Than street.

After lunch, walk over to Quan Thanh Temple before taking a leisurely stroll along West Lake. If you're up for it, you can follow the edge of Truc Bach lake or simply head straight to Tran Quoc Pagoda. It's possible to grab a coffee near here and admire West Lake from this vantage point, or to visit the bar at the Sofitel Plaza Hanoi for a more upscale environment. Grab dinner at bustling Xoi Yen in the Old Quarter before catching a cultural performance in the evening. Both the water puppet theater near Hoan Kiem Lake and a pair of *ca tru* (ancient chamber music) troupes hold regular shows throughout the week.

Vietnamese general Tran Hung Dao presides over the latter portion of the temple, tucked behind a high altar. Tran Hung Dao is credited with the defeat of two Mongol invasions, most famously in 1288, when he drove off Kublai Khan and his army after impaling their ships with wooden spikes. He is worshipped as one of the country's collective ancestors.

Ngoc Son houses a small exhibit on the turtles of Hoan Kiem Lake. Just one turtle remains in Hoan Kiem's murky green waters and sightings of the animal are rare.

Leading to Ngoc Son's entrance gate is a bright red footbridge, a popular photo spot.

On the far side of the path, look out for a relief of a tortoise on the left, carrying Le Thai To's famous sword. The area before Ngoc Son boasts nice views of Turtle Tower and the lake.

Hanoi Heritage House

Acting as both a tourist information center and an example of traditional Hanoian architecture, the Hanoi Heritage House (87 Ma May, 8:30am-noon and 1:30pm-5pm daily, VND10,000) is a long and narrow building stocked with a variety of Vietnamese handicrafts and helpful English explanations of each item's origin. The house hails from the late 19th century and is punctuated by a small, roofless courtyard, which provided ventilation.

Both levels are stocked with souvenirs, including Dong Ho folk paintings and ceramics, stone carvings, and other traditional wares. While it can feel like a shop, there's no pressure to purchase.

At the front desk are a few books outlining the history of the neighborhood and its many small streets, as well as their former purposes. Curious travelers can ask questions about the city. *Ca tru* (ancient chamber music) performances take place here a few times a week.

Bach Ma Temple

The oldest temple in Hanoi, 11th-century Bach Ma Temple (76 Hang Buom, 8am-11am and 2pm-5pm Tues.-Sun., free) may be modest in size but through its humble gates are inner walls drenched in red and gold, lacquered floor to ceiling, and intricate paintings and masterful woodwork. This tranquil hall honors deity Long Do, the chief of Hanoi's first settlement, who lived during the 4th century and is believed to have reappeared several times throughout Vietnamese history, particularly during conflicts with the Chinese, as a protector of the city and its people. Since he would sometimes appear in the form of a white horse, it is fitting that the temple's name translates to white horse. A large statue of a bright white stallion stands at the center of the building, surrounded by offerings and massive, gilded ironwood columns. Overhead, Bach Ma's collection of lintels (large lacquered wooden panels) featuring Chinese inscriptions, bear phrases such as "Thang Long's Guardian to the East" and "Indomitable Spirit of Heaven and Earth."

Temple caretakers typically break for lunch at midday. Visitors who turn up on the 1st or 15th of a lunar month are free to visit from morning to night, as these are special days in Vietnamese culture.

Long Bien Bridge

Long Bien Bridge (east of Tran Nhat Duat), a weathered iron structure, holds a special place in Hanoi's history. Completed in 1902 by French architects, the bridge was originally named after Indochina's governor general, Paul Doumer. It played a key role in both the Franco-Vietnam and American Wars. During the Viet Minh's fight against colonialism, rice and other supplies traveled across Long Bien to the troops at Dien Bien Phu, who defeated their French enemies in 1954. Through the 1960s and '70s the bridge served as a crucial link between Hanoi and the port city of Haiphong. As the only route across the Red River, Long Bien was bombed heavily during the American War and had to be rebuilt in 1973.

Only pedestrians and two-wheeled vehicles are permitted on the bridge. Nearby Chuong Duong Bridge serves as a link for trucks and other large vehicles.

Mosaic Mural

Running beneath Long Bien Bridge along Tran Nhat Duat, Hanoi's mosaic mural began as a project to commemorate the city's 1,000-year anniversary. It spans almost 2.5 miles along the western bank of the Red River, making it the longest ceramic wall in the world. Both local and foreign artists took part in the mosaic's creation, combining abstract pieces from international artists with several prominent Vietnamese symbols, such as a mosaic version of a Dong Son drum head and the ever-popular giant turtle of Hoan Kiem Lake carrying a sword on its back.

CATHEDRAL DISTRICT
St. Joseph's Cathedral

An imposing structure amid the narrow houses and one-room shops of downtown Hanoi, St. Joseph's Cathedral (40 Nha Chung, tel. 04/3825-4424, 5am-7am and 7pm-9pm daily, free) is one of the city's more recognizable landmarks, its pair of faded Gothic bell towers presiding over a small clearing just west of Hoan Kiem Lake. Originally the site of Bao Thien Pagoda, a Buddhist hall of worship dating as far back as the city itself, the church, built to resemble Paris's Notre

Cathedral District

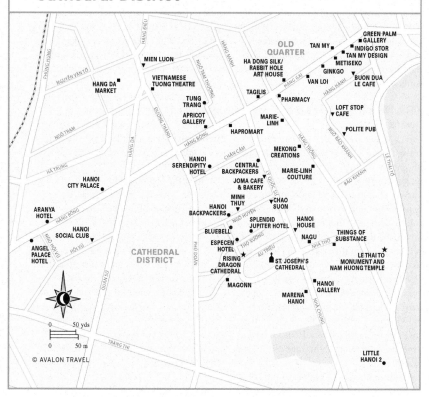

Dame Cathedral, opened in 1886 to a devout French parish. St. Joseph's remained open until the end of the American War, when the Communist government forbade religious gatherings. The cathedral reopened its doors in the early 1990s.

The modest square before the church, ringed by cafés and boutiques, boasts a statue of Mother Mary and is often busy in the late afternoons with students and locals. Though the front doors are usually closed, there is a side door by which visitors can enter to glimpse the brilliant red, white, and gold interior; most prefer to just take in the building from outside. Visitors can drop by the cathedral's English-language mass on Sundays at 11:30am if they feel so inclined.

Le Thai To Monument and Nam Huong Temple

Overlooking Hoan Kiem Lake, the towering **Le Thai To Monument** (Le Thai To, 8am-5pm daily, free) commemorates Le Thai To, the emperor who played a pivotal role in Vietnam's history and mythology. Also known as Le Loi, this 15th-century king defeated Chinese invaders with the help of a magical sword. Topped by a small statue of the emperor, the 1896 monument is well-preserved and vibrant, bordered by an array of blooms and large shade trees. A sturdy pavilion obscures the base of the memorial where incense and other offerings are laid.

Behind the statue, **Nam Huong Temple** honors the emperor and a handful of other deified citizens. It once served as a popular gathering place for writers, poets, and scholars, moving to its present location at the turn of the 20th century. While the temple is small (the width of the room is about five paces), the emperor's altar holds a riot of colorful offerings, decorative statues, and a few lacquered wooden tablets.

FRENCH QUARTER
Opera House

The capital's grand old Opera House (1 Trang Tien, tel. 04/3933-0113, www.hanoioperahouse.org.vn) is a stately structure overlooking the frenzied August Revolution Square. The theater, a yellow-and-white behemoth built in the colonial style, took a decade to complete, first opening its doors in 1911. Back then, only European performers were invited onto the stage and French colonists made up most of the audience. By 1940, Vietnamese citizens were able to rent out the massive hall, modeled after Paris's own opera house. When politics took center stage in 1945 and Vietnam declared its independence from the French, Hanoi's Opera House served as a meeting venue for gatherings of the new government.

Performances take place year-round. The opulent theater seats 598 spectators over three levels. Though visitors aren't permitted to wander around indoors, the exterior is worth a look while you're in the French Quarter.

National Museum of History and Revolutionary Museum

Housed in the former Louis Finot Museum, Vietnam's National Museum of History (1 Pham Ngu Lao, tel. 04/3824-1384, www.baotanglichsu.vn, 8am-noon and 1:30pm-5pm daily, VND40,000) showcases over 200,000 artifacts, documents, and historic relics. The main building is devoted to ancient civilizations such as the Sa Huynh, Oc Eo, and Champa, along with northern Vietnam's Dong Son, a culture which existed roughly in 1000 BC-AD 100 and whose large bronze drums are a symbol of Vietnam. Scores of artifacts, mostly stone implements, pottery, and jewelry, occupy the downstairs level, while the museum's upper floor packs in several centuries of dynastic rule, from the Dinh and Le eras of the AD 900s to Vietnam's last emperors, the Nguyen dynasty, whose ornate everyday items, from mother-of-pearl inlaid dressers to enamel jars, detailed ceramics, and vibrant lacquerware take up a display to themselves.

Despite a fair amount of English signage throughout the building, a lack of general historical information can leave non-Vietnamese speakers adrift.

Where the National Museum of History leaves off, with the text of Uncle Ho's famous declaration of independence, given at Ba Dinh Square on September 2, 1945, the Revolutionary Museum across the street picks up, with a slightly smaller range of documents, artifacts, and propaganda from the Franco-Vietnam and American Wars.

Entry to both museums is included in the ticket price, and visitors can spread out their visits over more than one day. There is a camera fee (VND15,000) to take photos within the museums. Both museums are closed the first Monday of the month.

Vietnamese Women's Museum

One of Hanoi's better offerings, the Vietnamese Women's Museum (36 Ly Thuong Kiet, tel. 04/3825-9936, www.baotangphunu.org.vn, 8am-5pm daily, VND30,000) takes a comprehensive look at the country's female citizens. Permanent exhibits cover everything from marriage and birth customs to family life, the crucial role of women in Vietnamese history, and the varied traditions practiced by ethnic minorities, all with ample English signage. A handful of temporary displays also pass through the modern, three-story building. The museum's clear organization places the museum a cut above many others in the city.

Hoa Lo Prison

In the heart of the French Quarter is a small

French Quarter

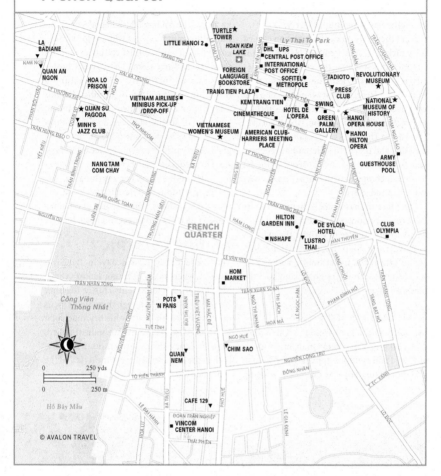

portion of **Hoa Lo Prison** (Hoa Lo and Hai Ba Trung, tel. 04/3824-6358, 8am-5pm daily, VND20,000, free for children under 15), the infamous jail that once housed thousands of Vietnamese revolutionaries during colonialism and, later, American prisoners of war. While most of the original complex has been demolished, the remainder of Hoa Lo serves as a museum, documenting its history and the struggles of its inmates.

Built by the French at the end of the 19th century, the facility then known as the Maison Centrale quickly surpassed its original 450-prisoner capacity, overflowing with nationalist Vietnamese who had rebelled against colonial rule. As many as 2,000 inmates were crammed in at one time, making for dismal conditions on top of the torture doled out by French prison guards. The museum holds ample evidence of these transgressions, including life-sized mannequins of Vietnamese prisoners, lined up and shackled at the feet, as well as a guillotine used by the colonial government during the early 20th century. Following the Franco-Vietnam and American Wars, several of Hoa Lo's inmates went on to serve as high-ranking officials in the Vietnamese Communist Party.

From the 1960s onward, the prison earned a new nickname. Dubbed the "Hanoi Hilton" by American soldiers, the complex was re-purposed by north Vietnamese forces for prisoners of war. Here, the story fractures into two separate accounts: that of its captives—including U.S. Senator John McCain, who spent over five years at Hoa Lo—who recall torture and brutality; and that of the Vietnamese government, which paints a rosy portrait of life on the inside, complete with Christmas dinners and organized sports.

The museum has a small memorial to its Vietnamese prisoners at the back of the complex. Visitors are free to wander the exhibits at their leisure. Skip the information booklets on sale at the ticket booth, as much of their text is featured on signs throughout the museum.

Quan Su Pagoda

Just south of Hoa Lo Prison, the wide yellow Quan Su Pagoda (Chua Quan Su, 73 Quan Su, 8am-11am and 1pm-4pm daily, free) is one of Hanoi's most popular centers of worship and is home to the Buddhist Association of Vietnam. Though it's not the city's oldest or even its most decorated pagoda, Quan Su, also known as the Ambassador's Pagoda, began in the 15th century as a guesthouse for visiting emissaries from Buddhist countries and has only grown since then. The current building was constructed in 1942 and features a dimly lit congregation of Buddha effigies on the main altar, a many-armed Quan Am, and a small section dedicated to local martyrs. Despite its downtown location, the pagoda courtyard is a peaceful place most days, though dozens gather here during religious festivals and holidays. For anything and everything Buddhism-related, check out the surrounding shops, where scores of religious books, relics, and other goods are sold.

BA DINH DISTRICT

You could easily pass a day in Ba Dinh District, where many of Hanoi's most prominent historical monuments cluster together south of West Lake. Though these sights focus on Vietnam's 20th-century history, much of it war-related or steeped in Communism, there are a few other worthy attractions in the area, such as the city's Museum of Fine Arts and the centuries-old Temple of Literature.

Ho Chi Minh Mausoleum

Ba Dinh District

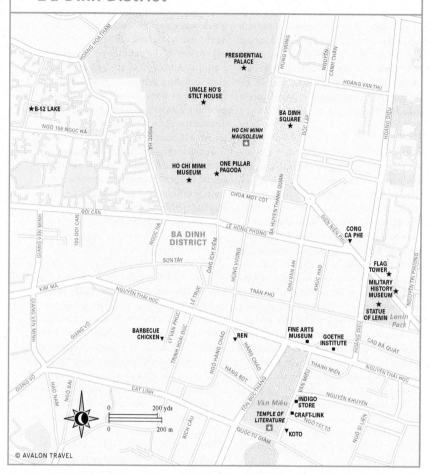

PRESIDENTIAL
PALACE
★

HOÀNG HOA THÁM

HÙNG VƯƠNG

NGUYỄN
CẢNH CHÂN

HOÀNG VĂN THỤ

UNCLE HO'S
STILT HOUSE
★

★ B-52 LAKE

NGÕ 158 NGỌC HÀ

NGỌC HÀ

BA DINH
SQUARE
★

HO CHI MINH
MAUSOLEUM
★

ĐỘC LẬP

HOÀNG DIỆU

HO CHI MINH
MUSEUM
★

ONE PILLAR
PAGODA
★

CHÙA MỘT CỘT

BÀ HUYỆN THANH QUAN

ĐỘI CẤN

100 ĐỘI CẤN

GIANG VĂN MINH

NGỌC HÀ

LÊ HỒNG PHONG

ĐIỆN BIÊN PHỦ

CONG
CA PHE
▼

BA DINH
DISTRICT

SƠN TÂY

ÔNG ÍCH KIỆM

HÙNG VƯƠNG

CHU VĂN AN

KHÚC HẠO

FLAG
TOWER
★

NGUYỄN TRI PHƯƠNG

MILITARY
HISTORY
MUSEUM
★

KIM MÃ

NGUYỄN THÁI HỌC

LÊ TRỰC

TRẦN PHÚ

STATUE
OF LENIN ★

Lenin
Park

GIANG VĂN MINH

GIANG VÕ

LÝ VĂN PHÚC

LÝ VĂN ĐỨC

BARBECUE
CHICKEN ▼

TRỊNH HOÀI ĐỨC

NGÕ HÀNG CHÁO

HÀNG CHÁO

▼ REN

FINE ARTS
MUSEUM ■

GOETHE
INSTITUTE ■

HOÀNG DIỆU

CAO BÁ QUÁT

NGUYỄN THÁI HỌC

HÀNG BỘT

THANH MIẾN

VĂN MIẾU

NGUYỄN KHUYỄN

GIANG VÕ

HÀO NAM

NGÕ BẢI

CAT LINH

TÔN ĐỨC THẮNG

Văn Miếu

■ INDIGO
STORE

NGÕ SI LIÊN

0   200 yds

0   200 m

BÍCH CÂU

TEMPLE OF
LITERATURE
★

QUỐC TỬ GIÁM

■ CRAFT-LINK

NGÕ TÁT TỐ

▼ KOTO

© AVALON TRAVEL

★ Ho Chi Minh Mausoleum

A stark stone cube occupying the western edge of massive Ba Dinh Square, the **Ho Chi Minh Mausoleum** (Ba Dinh Square, tel. 04/3845-5128, www.bqllang.gov.vn, 7:30am-10:30am Tues.-Thurs., 7:30am-11am Sat.-Sun. in summer, 8am-11am Tues.-Thurs., 8am-11:30am Sat.-Sun. in winter, free) bears only the words "President Ho Chi Minh" on its exterior. Guarded day and night by police in crisp white uniforms, this is perhaps one of Hanoi's most bizarre sights. On most mornings, dozens of local visitors line up to catch a glimpse of their leader's embalmed body. The swift, two-line procession moves indoors past one of Uncle Ho's most famous quotations—"Nothing is more precious than independence and freedom"—before gliding in a semi-circle around the body and back outside. Upon his death in 1969, Uncle Ho requested to be cremated and his ashes scattered in three parts throughout the north, south, and central regions of Vietnam, a wish that was obviously ignored.

Respectful dress is a must. Strict silence is observed indoors and no photography or camera equipment is permitted beyond the security checkpoint at the southern end of Ba Dinh Square, nor is the use of cell phones. Once you enter the line, it moves quickly, letting out on the opposite side of the building, where you can collect your electronics and carry on, either back out to the street or to any one of the Uncle Ho-related sights nearby.

Presidential Palace and Ho Chi Minh's Stilt House

Behind Ho Chi Minh's mausoleum, the **Presidential Palace** (1 Bach Thao, tel. 04/0804-4287, www.dutichhochiminhphuchutich.gov.vn, 7:30am-11am Mon.-Fri., 2pm-4pm Tues.-Thurs. in summer, 8am-11am Mon.-Fri., 1:30pm-4pm Tues.-Thurs. in winter, VND25,000) and his famous **stilt house** are remnants of both the French colonial government and its Communist successors. The bright, sunflower-hued palace, once home to the governor general of Indochina, served as both a private residence and administrative building for the colonial powers. Following Vietnam's independence, it was expected that Uncle Ho, as president, would move into the massive house. Instead, he converted the building into a solely political and administrative structure. The president made his home in a smaller structure nearby, now known as the 54 House, named after the year in which he moved in. This residence was short-lived.

At the same time, Ho Chi Minh commissioned a wooden stilt house, built in the style of Vietnam's ethnic minorities, where he lived for most of his remaining days. The modest, two-story building features an open ground floor, used for business, and sparsely furnished living quarters upstairs. The nearby fish pond and mango trees occupied much of the president's down time. A third and equally humble residence sits on the far side of the stilt house, completed in 1967 out of concern for Uncle Ho's well-being, as American bombs began to rain down on Hanoi in greater

numbers. Ho Chi Minh passed away here in September 1969.

Visitors can't access the Presidential Palace, which opens only for visiting heads of state. At the stilt house, you can only observe the upper floor of the building on an adjacent platform. A handful of artifacts are on display, including a few gifts presented to Ho Chi Minh by world leaders, as well as three gleaming antique cars used by the late president for travel, two of which were donated by the Soviet Union.

For more insight into this area, request a free English-speaking guide at the ticket booth. Guides are primarily university students who have taken the job to practice their language skills, so don't be surprised if the tour isn't terribly thorough.

Ho Chi Minh Museum

The gargantuan, lotus-shaped **Ho Chi Minh Museum** (19 Ngoc Ha, tel. 04/3846-3757, 8am-11:30am and 2pm-4pm Tues.-Thurs. and Sat.-Sun, 8am-11:30am Mon. and Fri.) is not the only Ho Chi Minh-related museum in Vietnam, but it is hands-down the biggest, packed with thousands of historical documents and artifacts, photographs, and exhibits on the life and achievements of the revolutionary leader. Over two floors, the museum's displays cover much of Uncle Ho's time abroad and his involvement in politics in France, China, and the United States, before his return to take up arms against the French. While there is heavy-handed Communist glorification and the English signage fails to offer big-picture synopses of Ho Chi Minh's life, it's a worthwhile attraction for history buffs. Before visiting, read even just a few paragraphs about Ho Chi Minh for a better appreciation of the exhibits.

One Pillar Pagoda

The short, squat **One Pillar Pagoda (Chua Mot Cot)** (6am-11am and 2pm-6pm daily, free) is dwarfed by the grand Communist monuments nearby, but it bears an interesting origin story. Standing at 13 feet high, the modest shrine, dedicated to Quan Am, is believed to date back to AD 1049, during the reign of emperor Ly Thai Tong. The legend goes that the inspiration for the pagoda came to the emperor in a dream, but there are conflicting versions of what the vision contained. Some say that the emperor dreamed of Quan Am sitting on a lotus blossom, holding a baby boy in her arms. The emperor, who wished for a son, became a father shortly thereafter and erected the monument as a thank-you to Quan Am. Given that Ly Thai Tong's son was born a few years before he ascended the throne in 1028, it doesn't seem likely that this version is correct.

The second version says that the emperor dreamed of Quan Am bringing him to a lotus lamp. Ly Thai Tong's mandarins worried that it was a bad omen. In an effort to counteract this negativity, the emperor commissioned the pagoda, paying homage to Quan Am.

The pagoda has undergone countless restorations and was rebuilt in 1249 and again in 1954, after the French destroyed it. Opposite the small shrine, **Dien Huu Pagoda** is a newer, more colorful building filled with a collection of statues and shrines that pairs nicely with a stroll up the steps of One Pillar.

The pagoda's proximity to Ho Chi Minh Museum and Ho Chi Minh Mausoleum makes it a frequent stop for visitors in Ba Dinh.

B-52 Lake

B-52 Lake (Ho Huu Tiep) (Ngo 158 Ngoc Ha or Ngo 55 Hoang Hoa Tham) sits amid a sleepy residential neighborhood, all but forgotten. Faded into Hanoi's everyday bustle, its tepid green waters serve as the backdrop for morning commutes, daily garbage collection, and the comings and goings of street vendors. Stretching up from the lake's surface is a stark reminder of the not-so-distant past: the mangled husk of a B-52 fighter jet, shot down during the 1972 Christmas bombings that rocked northern Vietnam. While much of the nearby landscape has changed, the lake remains frozen in time, a modest but powerful visual.

B-52 Lake elicits mixed reactions. For history and war buffs, it's a worthwhile stop paired with a visit to Ho Chi Minh Mausoleum and other surrounding sights. There is a simple plaque that stands at the near end of the water, and the plane's wreckage is surprisingly small.

To reach B-52 Lake you'll have to navigate several small alleys. Keep an eye out for signs that read "Ho B-52" or "Ho Huu Tiep" (the

altar outside of Dien Huu Pagoda

original name of the lake), as there are no English signs.

Military History Museum

The national Military History Museum (28A Dien Bien Phu, tel. 04/3823-4264, www. btlsqsvn.org.vn, 8am-11:30am and 1pm-4pm Tues.-Thurs. and Sat.-Sun., VND40,000) gathers various artifacts from Vietnam's two most prominent 20th-century wars, against French and American forces, within a bright white building. The indoor displays feature photos of the destruction that occurred.

The museum's outdoor exhibits provide more intrigue, with a sizable collection of military aircraft and ammunition, including one of the famous tanks that crashed through the gates of Saigon's Independence Palace on April 30, 1975, ending the American War. The museum highlights the cunning and resilience of a nation that, equipped with few resources, took on one of the world's most powerful armies and prevailed.

The grounds of the Military History Museum house Hanoi's red brick Flag Tower, a remnant of the imperial era built by emperor Gia Long in 1812. While it is possible to enter the tower and take the steps up to the highest of its platforms, those who pass on the museum can still see the monument from the street, and the photos are just as good, if not better, from here. The museum charges a camera fee (VND30,000), which includes the outdoor exhibits.

★ Temple of Literature

Hanoi's Temple of Literature (58 Quoc Tu Giam, tel. 04/3845-2917, 8am-5pm daily winter, 7:30am-5:30pm daily summer, VND20,000) hearkens back to AD 1070, when emperor Ly Thanh Tong ordered the construction of this temple complex. In 1076, emperor Ly Nhan Tong inaugurated Vietnam's first university, Quoc Tu Giam, on the long, rectangular grounds. The professors were court-appointed mandarins, who taught lessons on Confucianism, administration, literature, and poetry.

main gate at the Temple of Literature

While the university no longer stands, its grounds still hold an attractive garden, several lotus ponds, and the temple itself. Outside the main gate, a pair of stone engravings (in traditional Vietnamese characters) commands visitors to dismount from their horses. Through the imposing front door is a pleasant garden, filled with bright red flowers and frangipani trees. Lanterns line the central walkway that leads to the Khue Van pavilion, built in 1805, a tall, ornamental structure topped with bright red lacquered wood.

The temple's most famous attractions rest upon 82 giant stone tortoises, meant to symbolize wisdom and longevity. The 82 stelae honor Quoc Tu Giam's doctoral graduates listing 1,304 names. While you aren't allowed to wander through the rows of stelae, you can see the stone tablets up close.

The courtyard before the Temple of Literature once held altars for 72 of the most respected students to study under Confucius and, later, Chu Van An, a 13th-century scholar considered the father of Vietnamese education. The altar has been replaced with souvenir vendors hawking incense and a few interesting handicrafts.

The temple itself is divided into two sections. Under the first roof, a high altar sits in the open air, flanked by tortoise and crane statues. Everything from the ironwood columns to the gold Chinese inscriptions shines with a heavy lacquer, and incense fills the air. Beyond the high door—used to ensure entrants bow their heads in respect—is a large statue of Confucius and his disciples, dressed in lavish robes. A gold-plated ceramic tortoise sits to the left, while several smaller altars line the outskirts of the room.

Behind the temple are the original university grounds, now known as Thai Hoc courtyard. Completed in 2000, this area is dedicated to three Vietnamese emperors: Ly Thanh Tong, responsible for the original temple's construction, Ly Nhan Tong, founder of the national university, and Le Thanh Tong, the ruler who commissioned the first of the stelae.

While signage within the temple complex is fairly sparse, visitors can hire a guide (VND100,000) at the ticket booth or buy the information booklet (VND8,000). Though nothing beats a knowledgeable and enthusiastic guide, the booklet provides insight and historical background for a fraction of the cost.

WEST LAKE AREA
West Lake

North of the Old Quarter, West Lake (Ho Tay) is Hanoi's largest body of water and is a center for the city's wealthier residents. Ringed with luxury hotels and high-end restaurants, the lake once served as the northern frontier for Thang Long citadel. Of the legends related to the lake's origin, the most popular one goes that the area was once a forest, terrorized by a nine-tailed demon, which Lac Long Quan, original leader of the Vietnamese people, drowned in the waters of West Lake. Another story goes that an 11th-century monk by the name of Khong Lo traveled to China to aid the emperor and, as a reward for his services,

carried home large amounts of bronze. He used that bronze to make a bell with a sound so powerful that it confused a golden calf, who mistook the noise for its mother calling and, in his hurry to find her, created the deep rut that would form West Lake.

A narrow strip of land runs between West Lake and small Truc Bach. Though these two bodies of water were originally one, the southern lake received its own name after the completion of the Co Ngu causeway, upon which Tran Quoc Pagoda now sits. Truc Bach is remembered in Vietnam's war history as the site where, on October 26, 1967, American pilot John McCain parachuted into the water after his plane was shot down. Vietnamese civilians rescued the pilot before turning him in to Hoa Lo, where he spent over five years as a prisoner of war. A plaque near the lakeshore commemorates the event.

A trip to West Lake provides plenty of peace and quiet, and the lake boasts a 10-mile road around its shoreline, making for a scenic stroll or bike ride.

Tran Quoc Pagoda

One of Hanoi's oldest houses of worship, the Tran Quoc Pagoda (Thanh Nien/Co Ngu causeway, 7:30am-11:30am and 1:30pm-6:30pm daily, free) dates back to the 6th century, when its first incarnation was built on the banks of the Red River during the reign of emperor Ly Nam De. Its current home looks out over the gentle waters of West Lake and provides lovely views of the surrounding area.

Through a large yellow gate, the front half of Tran Quoc houses a collection of colorful stupas dwarfed by the 11-tiered tower at their center, which houses a ring of white Buddha statues on all sides. From this courtyard, visitors are able to peek in on the pagoda's ancestral altars, which line the wall of a shallow room off to the right. Farther back, a larger clearing houses a broad, leafy bodhi tree, gifted to the pagoda in 1959 by Indian president Rajendra Prasad. The bodhi tree carries special religious significance, as it was under this type of tree that the Sakyamuni Buddha

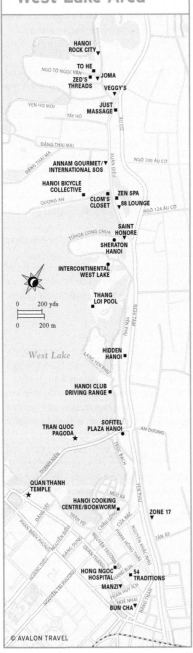

West Lake Area

HANOI
ROCK CITY
NGÕ TÔ NGỌC VÂN
TO HE
ZED'S
THREADS
JOMA
VEGGY'S
VEN HO MOI
TÂY HỒ
JUST
MASSAGE
ĐẶNG THAI MAI
ANNAM GOURMET/
INTERNATIONAL SOS
NGÕ 200 ÂU CƠ
HANOI BICYCLE
COLLECTIVE
QUONG AN
CLOM'S
CLOSET
ZEN SPA
88 LOUNGE
NGÕ 124 ÂU CƠ
TÙ HOA CONG CHÚA
SAINT
HONORE
SHERATON
HANOI
INTERCONTINENTAL
WEST LAKE
0   200 yds
0   200 m
THANG
LOI POOL
NGHI TÀM
YÊN PHỤ
West Lake
LÀNG YÊN PHỤ
HIDDEN
HANOI
HANOI CLUB
DRIVING RANGE
TRAN QUOC
PAGODA
SOFITEL
PLAZA HANOI
AN DƯƠNG
TRÚC BẠCH
THANH NIÊN
QUAN THANH
TEMPLE
HANOI COOKING
CENTRE/BOOKWORM
NGŨ XÃ
TRAN VU
CHÂU LONG
CỬA BẮC
ZONE 17
PHẠM HỒNG THÁI
TÂN ẤP
PHAN ĐÌNH PHÙNG
NGUYỄN BIỂU
ĐẶNG DUNG
NGUYỄN TRƯỜNG
QUÁN THÁNH
NGUYỄN KHẮC NHU
HÀNG ĐẬU
HOÀNG DIỆU
NGUYỄN TRI PHƯƠNG
HONG NGOC
HOSPITAL
HÀNG THAN
54
TRADITIONS
MANZI
PHAN HUY ÍCH
HÀNG THAN
HOÈ NHAI
BUN CHA
© AVALON TRAVEL

attained enlightenment in India. Another altar sits indoors, dedicated to Buddha and piled high with fruit offerings and lacquered ornamentation.

Quan Thanh Temple

As old as Hanoi itself, **Quan Thanh Temple** (corner of Quan Thanh and Thanh Nien, sunrise-sunset daily, VND10,000) was built in the 11th century under the reign of emperor Ly Thai To. Sitting just below West Lake, the temple honors Huyen Thien Tran Vu, protector of the city's northern gate, one of four directional deities who were believed to guard the Thang Long citadel in Hanoi's earliest days. The existing temple dates back to the 19th century and houses several precious antiques, including a 12-foot, four-ton statue of Tran Vu, cast in 1677, that takes up the back wall, as well as an oddly shaped gong from the 17th or 18th century. Through the temple's high white gate, a pair of stone elephants guard the courtyard leading up to Tran Vu's altar, lined with benches and large shade trees. Inside, lacquered woodwork decorates much of the shrine, while a photocopied map hangs on one of the building's columns, illustrating the parameters of Thang Long citadel and Quan Thanh Temple around 1490.

★ Vietnam Museum of Ethnology

Though it's removed from the rest of Hanoi's attractions, the **Vietnam Museum of Ethnology** (Nguyen Van Huyen, tel. 04/3756-2193, www.vme.org.vn, 8:30am-5:30pm Tues.-Sun., VND40,000) is worth a jaunt out to the western suburbs of the city. Opened in 1997, the large, round building, modeled after a Dong Son bronze drum, features exhibits on all 54 of Vietnam's ethnic communities, from the Kinh, or Vietnamese, who make up roughly 86 percent of the country's population, to dozens of minority groups, including the Cham, H'mong, Muong, Jarai, and Ede, many of whom live in the mountainous regions of northwestern and central Vietnam.

Ample signage guides visitors through the museum's vivid and educational exhibits, which cover customs, traditional dress, religion, architecture, farming techniques, handicrafts, and rituals practiced by each ethnicity. A small section on the 2nd floor organizes interactive activities for younger visitors, including traditional games and crafts.

Behind the building, several examples of traditional architecture are on display, including a stilted Ede longhouse and the soaring pitched roof of a Bahnar communal house, standing at 62 feet tall. **Water puppet performances** (10am, 11:30am, 2:30pm, and 4pm) take place several times a day in the pond nearby.

The museum is home to a small bookshop and souvenir store, as well as a café, run by the Hoa Sua School, an organization that trains disadvantaged Vietnamese youth. Book guided tours (VND100,000) ahead of time by calling the museum. There is also a camera fee (VND50,000) to take photos within the museum grounds.

To the right of the museum entrance is a building that curates a collection of cultural items from across Southeast Asia. Though still very much in its infancy, the Southeast Asian arm of the ethnology museum will feature the

same in-depth displays on customs, styles of dress, handicrafts, religions, and other facets of culture within Vietnam and its neighboring nations. It's worth a peek while you're here.

SIGHTSEEING TOURS

In a city as accessible as Hanoi, city tours aren't entirely necessary, as most travelers are able to hit their preferred points of interest alone. There are plenty of standard, generic city tours around town; skip these since they don't enhance your Hanoian experience. A handful of outfits in the capital excel at providing urban excursions with a more personal touch.

Founded in 2006, **Hanoi Kids** (tel. 09/7816-2283, www.hanoikids.org, 9am-5pm daily) is a free, student-run tour service that pairs curious travelers with young Vietnamese hoping to practice their English. All guides participate in regular training sessions before hitting the town with their new foreign friends, and your only costs as a traveler are admission fees and transportation for you and your guide. With equal give and take, these young Hanoians are enthusiastic and outgoing, making the experience feel more like a friendly outing than a run-of-the-mill tour. Due to the popularity of the group, reserving

Chinese characters adorn the entrance of Quan Thanh Temple.

a spot ahead of time is a must. The booking department at Hanoi Kids sometimes needs a reminder. Confirm your tour in advance and, if response seems slow, give the office a call and check in.

A popular and reliable operator for tours both in town and around northern Vietnam, Adventure Indochina (1 Hang Buom, tel. 04/6683-5539, www.adventureindochina.com, 8am-8pm daily) arranges trips to Ha Long Bay and Sapa in addition to running city tours of Hanoi, cyclo excursions, a one-day journey focused around the city's pagodas, and a tasty street food tour. Staff are knowledgeable and efficient, and prices tend toward the more affordable end of the spectrum.

Just over two miles north of the Old Quarter, Hidden Hanoi (147 Nghi Tam, tel. 09/1225-4045, www.hiddenhanoi.com.vn, 9am-5pm daily Mon.-Sat., VND420,000-945,000) introduces travelers to the finer points of Vietnamese culture through food, language, and walking adventures around the city. Its popular cooking classes take place at the center's charming location on the eastern edge of West Lake, as do a handful of language courses. Several walking tours around the Old and French Quarters take place downtown along with a much-touted street food tour. Prices vary depending upon the activity, but all guides are enthusiastic and knowledgeable, making these tours a worthy investment.

Entertainment and Events

NIGHTLIFE

As the sun sets over the capital, Hanoi's nightlife festivities take place in fast-forward, unraveling in a few short hours between sundown and midnight. By 6pm or 7pm, work has barely let out but locals line the streets, gathering on clusters of low, plastic stools to enjoy fresh beer and *do nhau* (drinking food), as they rehash the day's events. An hour later, nightlife is in full swing, with droves of foreigners and Vietnamese packed onto the makeshift furniture of so many independent beer vendors, noshing on grilled meat or snails, a local favorite, washed down with any one of the country's local brews. The streets of the Old Quarter are especially lively, drawing people from all walks of life.

Across town, the well-heeled pay a visit to swanky cocktail lounges and upmarket watering holes around West Lake and throughout the French Quarter, where top-shelf spirits, terrace seating, and mellow mood music speak to a more refined ambience, while the catch-all bar-and-restaurants near St. Joseph's Cathedral sling cheap beers and other beverages in a casual, laid-back environment. Wherever you are, the night reaches its peak around 9pm, and from there things run on their own steam until midnight, when a fairly strict curfew is enforced and most businesses close their doors for the evening. A handful of bars quietly remain open for another hour or so.

There is hope for late-night revelers. As a city that prides itself very much on traditional values, Hanoi has been resistant to progress on the nightlife front, but several business owners attempted to push the envelope recently. During the second half of 2013, a short-lived but influential neighborhood known as Zone 9, situated a mile south of Hoan Kiem Lake, gave rise to a promising flourish of artistic and cultural venues, but it was promptly and inexplicably shut down by local police only a few months later. While the blow was a setback to Hanoi's after-dark scene, it made an impression on young locals and expats, offering a hopeful glimpse of the city's late-night future.

Bars

Dimly lit and heavily outfitted in red lacquered woodwork, the lovable, laid-back Mao's Red Lounge (7 Ta Hien, tel. 04/3926-3104,

Hanoi's Craft Beer Scene

As the workday comes to a close and an army of motorbikes floods the city streets, the place to be in the capital is a small plastic chair by the roadside with an ice-cold glass of *bia hoi* in hand. This light, refreshing lager is a staple of northern nightlife, drawing crowds to the bustling sidewalks of downtown Hanoi on a daily basis. What sets this particular brew apart is its makeup: Local breweries concoct the amber liquid using basic beer ingredients like hops, yeast, and rice. Without any preservatives or additional chemicals, the beer's shelf life becomes especially brief, with most *bia hoi* unfit to drink by the end of the night. Local establishments must plan ahead, ordering just enough to last a single day. In the wee hours of the morning, a representative goes to the brewery to pick up an order of *bia hoi*. From the time it reaches the premises, shopkeepers work to unload as

tourists and locals enjoying *bia hoi*

much of their stock as possible, slinging drinks throughout the day, but the rush comes in the evenings, when Hanoi's sidewalks come alive and a healthy drinking culture helps to push sales along. *Bia hoi* is often enjoyed with street-side snacks, known as *do nhau* in Vietnamese. The brew comes in at roughly four percent alcohol by volume, making it a highly drinkable beverage, if a little watery. Best of all, its price tag runs no higher than VND5,000 in the big city, making it far and away the most affordable beverage around. You can also look for the slightly more expensive *bia tuoi*, a similar recipe with a bit more flavor. Both varieties are commonly translated as "fresh beer."

There are many *bia hoi* shops in downtown Hanoi. The most popular is often referred to as **bia hoi corner** (corner of Ta Hien and Luong Ngoc Quyen, 10am-midnight daily, VND5,000/glass). While not all of the corner shops serve genuine *bia hoi*, you'll find plenty of the brew on the southeast edge of the junction. Beyond this swarm of nighttime activity, a clutch of more locally frequented *bia hoi* are situated around Bat Dan and Duong Thanh near the western side of the Old Quarter, though you won't find any English speakers here. For a more detailed list of the many *bia hoi* watering holes, the Hanoi Bia Hoi's website (www.squeakieice.com/hanoi-bia-hoi) offers a helpful interactive map that covers the most popular *bia hoi* locations in Hanoi's five main districts.

5pm-midnight daily, VND25,000-80,000) is staffed by a friendly crowd and offers reasonable prices on beer, wine, and cocktails. Barside seating, low tables, and a few outdoor spots afford drinkers their pick of atmosphere. The place usually sees at least a steady trickle of visitors in the evenings.

Another laid-back backpacker hangout, **The Coach House** (37 Dao Duy Tu, tel. 09/1204-1416, 4pm-midnight daily, VND20,000-70,000) offers daily drink specials on its range of beer and cocktails. Grab a seat indoors, where contemporary music and walls full of photos give personality to the space, along with its comfy seating and an

array of cobbled-together wooden furniture, or stay outside, enjoying your evening from a low table just beyond the door. The place never gets truly busy, but it has a fun crowd of regulars and an easygoing atmosphere.

True to its name, the **Polite Pub** (5B Bao Khanh, tel. 00/0419-8086, 5pm-midnight daily, VND35,000-150,000) serves as a slightly more upscale watering hole than some of its Old Quarter competition farther north without getting too pretentious. Tucked down a quiet street off Hoan Kiem Lake, the cozy venue serves a list of beer, wine, spirits, and cocktails. Ample seating is available up front, while a pool table occupies the back room.

Lounges

A cozy street-side lounge not far from the Opera House, Tadioto (24B Tong Dan, tel. 04/6680-9124, 9am-midnight daily, VND35,000-270,000) exudes a laid-back vibe with plush couches, leather bar stools, and bright red French doors in a prime people-watching neighborhood. Prices are reasonable and a happy hour drink looking out onto Tong Dan is worthwhile. The bar boasts an assortment of beer, wine, and cocktails.

From a rooftop in the French Quarter, Hanoi's chic and sophisticated Press Club (59A Ly Thai To and 12 Ly Dao Thanh, tel. 04/3934-0888, www.hanoi-pressclub.com, 7am-10:30pm daily, VND95,000-300,000) affords pleasant views of one of the city's most upscale neighborhoods as well as a range of signature cocktails, top-shelf spirits, wine, and beer. Seating is available indoors at the Press Club's elegant bar or outside on a breezy, palm-fringed terrace. Live music acts occasionally pop up here, while regular drink specials, like the Thursday buy-two-get-one-free deal, run throughout the week.

The swanky and sophisticated 88 Lounge (88 Xuan Dieu, tel. 04/3718-8029, www.88group.vn, 11am-midnight daily, VND50,000-400,000) overlooks West Lake, with three floors of open-air seating that afford top-notch views of the water from an array of antique upholstered chairs. Pair this with dim lighting, a well-stocked downstairs bar, and an impressive collection of fine wines on display and the place is a hit, functioning as one of the neighborhood's best stand-alone lounges. Prices are steep, but these folks know their wines, not to mention everything else, from whiskey and scotch to soju, sake, and tequila.

Clubs

Loud, lively, and filled with nonstop energy, Dragonfly (15 Hang Buom, tel. 09/3699-3557, 7pm-midnight daily, VND40,000-100,000) is a small Hanoian version of a nightclub, slipped between the shops along Hang Buom. Those looking for a spot to let loose on the dance floor will appreciate the up-tempo beats and cheap drinks. For a slightly quieter atmosphere, head to the second floor, though don't expect to leave here without at least a little hearing damage.

When all the other bars have closed and the rest of Hanoi is calling it a night, the fun begins at Zone 17 (17D Hong Ha, tel. 09/7843-5453, 9pm-6am daily, VND30,000-100,000), a rare after-hours venue in a city where midnight curfew is heavily enforced. Sporting exposed brick walls and bamboo furnishings, the spacious bar holds regular events, including guest DJs and the occasional live music performance. Even on quiet evenings, a cheerful atmosphere and a steady stream of nighttime revelers keep the place busy. Though Zone 17 opens its doors at 9pm, time your visit later in the evening, as the party doesn't really get underway before midnight.

Live Music

Every evening from 9pm, the second floor of the Hotlife Cafe on Quan Su becomes Minh's Jazz Club (65 Quan Su, tel. 04/3942-0400, www.minhjazzvietnam.com, 9pm-midnight daily, VND60,000-200,000), a loud and lively lounge that showcases the best of Hanoi's jazz talent. Self-taught saxophonist and accomplished musician Quyen Van Minh, the club's owner, has cultivated an appreciation of jazz in the city, drawing nightly crowds into the intimate café for an impressive live performance. No cover charge is required, though prices double at showtime to accommodate for the musicians.

Bright and eye-catching, the main entrance of Swing (21 Trang Tien, tel. 04/3824-5395, www.swinglounge.com.vn, 7am-midnight daily, VND35,000-190,000) is decked out in high-wattage light bulbs, announcing this chic musical venue from a block away. Though it moonlights as an upscale café for the business crowd during the day, the lounge is at its best after dark, when the entire black-and-white space is transformed by nightly performances. The usual beer, wine, and cocktails are on offer, as well as non-alcoholic café beverages, and cozy sofa seating is scattered throughout. Music begins at 9pm and runs until closing time.

Buried down an alley north of West Lake, Hanoi Rock City (27/52 To Ngoc Van, tel. 018/8748-7426, www.hanoirockcity.com, 4pm-midnight Sun.-Thurs., 4pm-3am Fri.-Sat., VND50,000-200,000) continues to make its mark on Hanoi's live music scene as one of the premier venues for both local and international artists to showcase their talent. Boasting a spacious interior as well as a sprawling garden area, the funky West Lake venue also hosts the occasional DJ or film screening and keeps a regular list of upcoming acts on its website and Facebook page. Events usually include a cover charge, though it's never more than VND100,000.

THE ARTS

Hanoi boasts a glut of Vietnam's most talented artists, from musicians and photographers to lacquer painters, sculptors, and masters of traditional theater and puppetry. Scores of small, independent galleries and cultural centers exist alongside more formal institutions like the national Museum of Fine Arts and Hanoi's imposing Opera House. Even cafés and a few other small venues have gotten in on the city's arts and culture scene with small film screenings, ongoing exhibitions, artist talks, and other events. For the most up-to-date information, keep an eye on *The Word* (www.wordhanoi.com), whose online and print editions include an events calendar with upcoming shows, concerts, exhibitions, and other performances, as well as Hanoi Grapevine (www.hanoigrapevine.com), another reliable event-listing site.

Performing Arts

For everything from ballet to orchestral music, jazz concerts, piano recitals, operas, and traditional Vietnamese theater, Hanoi's historic Opera House (1 Trang Tien, tel. 04/3933-0113, www.hanoioperahouse.org.vn, box office: 8am-5pm daily) is the go-to venue.

The talented musicians of the Hanoi Ca

Tru Club (42-44 Hang Bac, tel. 09/8967-9829, www.catru.vn, 8pm Wed., Fri., and Sun., VND210,000) put on thrice-weekly performances in the heart of the Old Quarter. In a small, intimate space, the 70-minute show celebrates *ca tru*, a centuries-old form of northern Vietnamese poetry set to music, typically featuring one female singer, a male instrumentalist, and a drummer. While the traditional music is well-known throughout the Red River Delta area, *ca tru* is something of a dying art, as most of its musicians are older and the dwindling number of performers have made *ca tru* troupes harder to come by in modern times. Today, accomplished musicians keep the tradition alive through regular shows, usually for foreign visitors. Each performance features a small audience and often requires participation on the part of the attendees. Hanoi Ca Tru Club does a nice job of providing background information on the musical traditions of the north as well as how to join in.

Tickets can be purchased throughout the week, with typical box office hours (8am-5pm), though you'll still be able to snag a seat on the evening of a performance, provided there are spots available. Book your ticket a day in advance. If you can't finagle a seat with the Hanoi Ca Tru Club, you can also try the Thang Long Ca Tru Club (87 Ma May, tel. 012/2326-6897, www.catruthanglong.com, 8pm Tues., Thurs., and Sat., VND210,000), another well-known local troupe.

The vivacious characters of Thang Long Water Puppet Theater (57B Dinh Tien Hoang, tel. 04/3824-9494, www.thanglongwaterpuppet.org, 1:45pm-9:15pm daily, VND100,000) know how to make a splash, zipping across their watery stage several times a day at Hanoi's best-known *mua roi* (water puppet) venue. As early as the 11th century, rice paddies and other shallow waters in the Red River Delta served as performance spaces for these lacquered wooden puppets and their masters, who maneuver the characters from behind a bamboo screen. Nowadays, the performances, combined with lively voice actors and traditional Vietnamese music are a popular cultural attraction for visitors to the city. Each show runs around 50 minutes, featuring a handful of individual vignettes. While the performance takes place in Vietnamese, the watery antics of these puppets provide enough information that no translation is necessary.

Museums

Spread over three floors, exhibits at the city's Museum of Fine Arts (66 Nguyen Thai Hoc, tel. 04/3823-3084, www.vnfam.vn, 8:30am-5pm daily, VND30,000) cover the creative achievements of Vietnamese painters, sculptors, and other craftspeople from the 11th century onward. Beginning with the stone and wood carvings of several of Vietnam's early dynasties, displays proceed chronologically through the country's artistic development, showcasing beautiful functional pieces and religious relics from the earliest days of the empire before carrying on to the 19th- and 20th-century fusion of Western ideas and materials with Vietnamese aesthetics. The resulting artwork, which includes vivid lacquer paintings alongside other mediums, like oil and acrylic, remains straightforward, depicting everyday Vietnamese scenes, portraits, and still life renderings. The most recent paintings hail from the 1980s and '90s. Its sole showroom of conceptual art is a letdown. The museum overall is a rewarding stop on your tour of the city and remains intriguing for both its artwork and the visible evolution of ideas over the years. Visitors are free to explore the many rooms of this 1930s colonial building on their own; a handy map is provided upon arrival that helps guide you through the museum's many numbered exhibits.

One part art space, one part café, the hip and happening Manzi (14 Phan Huy Ich, tel. 04/3716-3397, 9am-midnight daily) sits a few blocks beyond the Old Quarter and hosts regular art exhibitions, talks, film screenings, and music and dance performances within its updated French colonial digs. White walls and minimal furniture give the place a gallery feel. Visitors are invited to sit and enjoy the café, either downstairs amid the calm of alley life or upstairs with the art. Both international and Vietnamese artists have been featured in Manzi's two-story space, and its rotating schedule of cultural performances and events is updated regularly on Facebook.

Located just behind the Temple of Literature and a short walk from the Museum of Fine Arts, Hanoi's Goethe Institute (56-58 Nguyen Thai Hoc, tel. 04/3734-2251, www.goethe.de, 9am-7pm daily) remains an active part of the local art scene, holding regular exhibits, workshops, and film screenings in its DOCLAB. Many of these events are free and open to the public. Check out the institute's website or Facebook page for a list of upcoming exhibitions.

The pristine white walls of Green Palm Gallery (15 Trang Tien, tel. 04/3936-4757, www.greenpalmgallery.com, 8am-8pm daily) display some of Hanoi's top contemporary talents, such as Nguyen Thanh Binh, Nguyen The Dung, and Nguyen Manh Hung. With a layout that pays homage to traditional Vietnamese architecture, paintings and sculptures are spread out over three rooms, separated at the center by a small courtyard. Each piece is given its due space, and knowledgeable employees are on hand to answer questions. The gallery also has a second location (39 Hang Gai, tel. 09/1321-8496, 8am-8pm daily) closer to downtown, but the Trang Tien branch offers more peace and quiet.

Rabbit Hole Art House (102 Hang Gai, 2nd Fl., tel. 04/3928-5056, www.rabbithole-arthouse.com, 8am-8pm daily) is a modest space where a collective of young, up-and-coming Hanoian artists displays its masterpieces. Crossing a variety of mediums, from sculpture and oil painting to lacquer and ink illustrations, this one-room gallery offers a window into Hanoi's contemporary art scene.

With a laundry list of featured artists, the Apricot Gallery (40B Hang Bong, tel. 04/3828-8965, www.apricotgallery.com.vn, 8am-8pm daily) is one of Hanoi's most established showrooms, bringing together a variety of materials and aesthetic styles under one roof. Paintings tend to be oil or acrylic, though there are a few lacquer works here, too, and the long, narrow exhibit space, which extends a few floors up above, offers plenty to admire as you wander from room to room.

Cinema

For a dose of Western culture, the local CGV (6th Fl. Vincom Center, 191 Ba Trieu, tel. 04/3974-3333, www.cgv.vn, 8am-midnight daily, VND100,000-115,000) movie theater plays Hollywood blockbusters in English and features all your usual cinematic accoutrements, including a concession stand, 3D glasses, and Dolby digital. Tickets can be purchased at the theater or online.

Buried behind the stocky, square-shaped buildings that run unbroken along Hai Ba Trung, Cinematheque (22A Hai Ba Trung, tel. 04/3936-2648, 7pm and 9pm daily, VND60,000) is Hanoi's only art-house cinema. A happy departure from your average trip to the movies, this independent film club hosts daily screenings that run the spectrum from classic films to documentaries, independent shorts, and beyond. Outside the viewing room, a small bar sits in its interior courtyard, removed from the street noise and dotted with plants, while the theater-style seating indoors makes for a genuine cinematic experience without the crowds and noise of a local

movie theater. Showings take place at 7pm and 9pm each night; these times can fluctuate, occasionally opting for just one showing at 7pm. Call ahead and inquire about movies and screening times. While Cinematheque is technically a members-only club, first-time visitors are able to join once, provided they pay the mandatory donation fee.

FESTIVALS AND EVENTS

While this celebration sweeps across the whole country, Hanoi's festivities during the Mid-Autumn Festival (early-mid Sept.) are especially lively. The holiday, which falls on the 15th day of the eighth lunar month, typically takes place during the first half of September and features scores of colorful decorations. Brightly hued paper lanterns hang from every shop and house in the city, many of them originating from Hang Ma, which becomes the city's very own *pho long den* (lantern street) in the weeks leading up to the celebration. Running the gamut from traditional red-and-yellow lanterns to cartoon-shaped paper torches, shops along this narrow Old Quarter road do big business for the holiday, as local families, many of them with young children, partake in the festivities with paper lanterns and moon cake *(banh trung thu)*, a round, dense pastry whose reputation is not unlike fruitcake at Christmastime: pretty, ornamental, and not nearly as delicious as it looks.

Shopping

Hanoi's compact and chaotic Old Quarter is a microcosm of dressmakers and tailors, craftspeople, carpenters, souvenir vendors, and galleries. One-stop convenience may elude the city's busy streets, but avid shoppers will appreciate the Hanoian retail experience, stumbling upon small, charming boutiques and modest, out-of-the-way shops, each bringing its own unique personality to the multifaceted

neighborhood. Independent designers and skilled artisans display their finest wares, often at a price, while mass-produced items like T-shirts, buttons, and hats fill the narrow crevices between buildings, allowing travelers of all budgets to partake in Hanoi's commercial streets. While most of the city's downtown businesses use price tags, the cost of common souvenirs is negotiable wherever you are.

MARKETS

Dong Xuan Market

The sprawling Dong Xuan Market (Dong Xuan and Cau Dong, tel. 04/3828-2170, www.dongxuanmarket.com.vn, 6am-6pm daily), just west of Long Bien Bridge, packs everything under the sun into its two-story shelter. The French-built trading center is a Hanoian institution, famous for its array of products and so popular that it has spilled out onto the streets, turning the road in front of the building into a lively shopping area that becomes the city's night market after dark. Expect to find cheap souvenirs, along with countless bolts of fabric, T-shirts, and many other items.

Hom Market

For fabric shopping, Hom Market (Pho Hue, sunrise-sunset daily) just south of Hoan Kiem Lake is the go-to venue, lined with stall upon stall of materials at bargain prices. The usual market items are sold here, from food and household products to shoes, clothing, and other goods, but the real reason to venture into its maze of vendors is the innumerable bolts of fabric. Be sure to haggle, as Hom Market's shrewd businesswomen can drive a hard bargain.

Night Market

Hanoi's regular night market (Hang Dao north to Dong Xuan Market, 7pm-midnight Fri.-Sun.) runs from the end of Hang Dao north all the way to Dong Xuan Market, turning the road into a pedestrian-only affair flush with shops selling clothing, dry goods, and souvenirs. Be sure to haggle on this road, as prices tend to start high. Purchasing multiple items can usually get you a discount. While the bazaar only takes place on weekends, many vendors still set up smaller versions of their street stalls on the other days of the week.

SHOPPING DISTRICTS

Trang Tien

Wedged between the southern end of Hoan Kiem Lake and the Red River a few blocks to the east, Trang Tien is Hanoi's luxury shopping neighborhood, replete with high-end fashion, international brands, and familiar designer labels. Ply the narrow streets that spider off August Revolution Square, and you'll discover droves of art galleries, swanky boutiques, and posh cafés.

Running the length of a city block, Trang Tien Plaza (corner of Dinh Tien Hoang and Trang Tien, tel. 04/3937-8600, www.

the enormous Dong Xuan Market

The Clothes Make the Traveler

Though much of Hanoi is a retail paradise for women's clothing, it can be hard to know where to start your shopping adventure. The Old Quarter, particularly around Hang Gai and Hang Bong, is chock-full of high-quality brands like Tan My Design (61 Hang Gai, tel. 04/3825-1579, www.tanmydesign.com, 8am-8pm daily), Ha Dong Silk (102 Hang Gai, tel. 04/3928-5056, hadong-silks@gmail.com, 8am-8pm daily), and Metiseko (71 Hang Gai, tel. 04/3935-2645, www.metiseko.com, 8:30am-9pm daily). A handful of standouts in the Cathedral District are worth a visit, such as Marie-linh (74 Hang Trong, tel. 04/3928-6304, www.marie-linh.com, 9am-8pm daily) and Magonn (19 Ma May, tel. 04/3935-1811, www.magonn.vn, 9am-9pm daily). Much of the clothing on offer is made with Vietnamese sizes in mind. Those who are larger than the average Vietnamese woman may want to check out shops like Things of Substance (5 Nha Tho, tel. 04/3828-6965, www.prieure.com.vn, 9am-9pm daily) or the tailors in the Old Quarter or West Lake. For more formal, one-of-a-kind items, a trip to Chula (6 Ven Ho Tay, tel. 09/0425-8960, www.chulafashion.com, 9am-6:30pm daily) is highly advised.

For budget shoppers, the long road (known as Hang Dao, Hang Ngang, or Hang Duong at different points) leading from Hoan Kiem Lake to Dong Xuan Market holds a host of clothing and souvenir shops, as does the intersection where Hang Dao and Hang Gai connect. Shops like Ginkgo (79 Hang Gai, tel. 04/3938-2265, www.ginkgo-vietnam.com, 8am-10pm daily) and Orange (36 Luong Ngoc Quyen, tel. 04/3935-1387, www.orangestyle.vn, 9am-10pm daily) offer affordable T-shirts and bags, while Tagilis (12 Hang Bong, tel. 04/3990-7088, www.tagilis.wordpress.com, 9am-9pm daily) is an affordable tailor option. Retail outfits along the Old Quarter's Ma May and Ngo Huyen in the Cathedral District also carry the standard array of souvenirs, T-shirts, casual pants, and sundresses.

The options for men's clothing are fewer and limited to standard shirts and shorts. Keep an eye out for the minimal offerings in local boutiques. The streets south of Hoan Kiem Lake toward Hom Market hold a handful of more exciting men's options, as does Zed's Threads (51A To Ngoc Van, tel. 09/4753-6515, www.zedsthreads.com, 10am-6pm daily) in West Lake, though none of these are unique to Vietnam, but are instead a more affordable version of what you might find at home.

---

trangtienplaza.vn, 9:30am-9:30pm Mon.-Fri., 9:30am-10pm Sat.-Sun.) houses several international luxury brands, including Bulgari, Cartier, Estee Lauder, and Lancome, along with designer labels such as Louis Vuitton, Dior, and Versace, over six floors. The center was first built in 1901 to accommodate the city's French colonial shoppers. Its current incarnation opened to the public in 2013 as Hanoi's first luxury shopping center.

The Foreign Language Bookstore (64 Trang Tien, tel. 04/3825-7376, 8am-8pm daily), just down the road from Trang Tien Plaza, stocks recent American and European magazines such as *Time, Elle, The Economist* and *Marie-Claire*, along with the usual government-approved collection of English-language classics. The shop's section of Vietnam-related books slowly gives

way to a cache of souvenir items and road and city maps.

Old Quarter

Squeezed into an impossibly small neighborhood north of the lake, Hanoi's historic Old Quarter offers some of the best and most diverse shopping in the city, with stores to fit every budget and taste. From sleek, well-crafted furniture to eye-catching independent boutiques, traditional handicrafts, dime-a-dozen souvenirs, and the odd art gallery, Hang Gai and its nearby lanes represent the bulk of the area's offerings. There is also the occasional shop slipped between restaurants and hotels around Ma May, as well as a few of the more affordable souvenir shops buried within the backpacker alley off Ly Quoc Su near the cathedral. Head down sleepy Au

The Streets of the Old Quarter

In centuries past, each narrow road in the Old Quarter carried a specific product. Hang Quat, for instance, sold fans, or *quat*, while Hang Giay made its money from paper, or *giay*. Cha Ca was where you went to buy grilled fish, silver was on Hang Bac, and Hang Duong held much of the city's sugar supply. Today, many of these streets have changed trades. Hang Dau, the former oil street, now specializes in shoes, for instance. But, the traditional names have stuck.

Trieu on either side of St. Joseph's, and the hip clothing stores and independent labels reappear.

For fun, colorful, Vietnam-inspired T-shirts, both Orange (36 Luong Ngoc Quyen, tel. 04/3935-1387, www.orangestyle. vn, 9am-10pm daily) and Ginkgo (79 Hang Gai, tel. 04/3938-2265, www.ginkgo-viet-nam.com, 8am-10pm daily) offer well-made, affordable men's and women's threads with more originality than the stock souvenir items around town. Ginkgo also has a second location (44 Hang Be, tel. 04/3926-4769, 8am-10pm daily) removed from the frenzy of Hang Gai.

Branding itself as eco-chic women's clothing, Metiseko (71 Hang Gai, tel. 04/3935-2645, www.metiseko.com, 8:30am-9pm daily) combines organic cotton, all-natural silk, and other eco-friendly fabrics with bright, solid colors and Vietnamese-inspired prints to create designs with a whimsical feel. All fabrics meet Global Organic Textile standards. The store also features a smaller selection of children's clothing and home goods. Western-level prices apply here, but the thought and quality put into Metiseko's offerings justify their cost.

Pairing the roaring 1920s with vibrant, edgy prints and colors, Magonn (19 Ma May, tel. 04/3935-1811, www.magonn.vn, 9am-9pm daily) brings an old-world class to its chic, modern style. The well-stocked hipster boutique features a line of original women's clothing created by a young, Hanoi-based design duo, running the gamut from classy to casual with sleek pencil skirts, flirty A-line frocks, and drop-waist dresses.

The smart, understated clothing at Indigo Stor (47 Hang Gai, tel. 04/3938-1859, www. indigo-store.com, 8am-8pm daily) may not jump out at you, but the beauty of these items lies in their simplicity. Using traditional methods, the shop sticks to indigo-dyed clothing for both men and women, using all-natural fabrics and embroidery courtesy of Vietnam's ethnic minorities, whose colorful, intricate needlework jumps out from the plain blue background.

One of a few skilled tailors on the block, Ha Dong Silk (102 Hang Gai, tel. 04/3928-5056, hadongsilks@gmail.com, 8am-8pm daily) fashions high-quality custom items. The shop also boasts a range of ready-made women's clothing along with accessories and jewelry. The ground floor of the building houses off-the-rack options; the fabric selection is upstairs.

The two floors of local favorite Tan My Design (61 Hang Gai, tel. 04/3825-1579, www.tanmydesign.com, 8am-8pm daily) are a catchall of jewelry, accessories, women's clothing, and housewares, run by three generations of a Hanoian family. From dresses to necklaces, bags, and bedding, Tan My pairs bright, bold colors with a distinctly Vietnamese flair, drawing upon the best of the old and the new. There is a small black-and-white café in the back of the narrow, all-white store. Across the street is Tan My's original location (66 Hang Gai, tel. 04/3825-1579, www.tanmyembroi-dery.com.vn, 8am-8pm daily), which specializes in beautiful hand-embroidered silks and other fabrics.

Perhaps the most affordable tailor on the block, Tagilis (12 Hang Bong, tel.

04/3990-7088, www.tagilis.wordpress.com, 9am-9pm daily) specializes in well-made women's dresses in a range of materials and styles. The cheerful folks who run the shop are willing to copy designs or come up with new ones, and the average knee-length dress should set you back around VND670,000, give or take a few dollars depending upon the cut and fabric. Ready-made items are also available in bright colors and prints.

A long, narrow shop squeezed between the tailors and silk vendors of Hang Gai, Van Loi (87 Hang Gai, tel. 04/3828-6758, www.vanloi.com, 8am-7pm daily) does a trade in beautiful wooden furniture, mother-of-pearl dishware, lacquer trays, and other home furnishings. Colorful or traditional, ostentatious or reserved, all items are produced locally and with care. The shop's smaller kitchen items and decorative pieces make easy-to-pack souvenirs.

Cathedral District

A less hectic extension of the Old Quarter, Hanoi's Cathedral District is home to a handful of unique, creative boutiques selling women's clothing, ceramics, and other knick-knacks. Prices are a little more reasonable here, away from the main shopping drag. This area is still well within the bounds of Hanoi's more touristy area, so expect to find plenty of foreign shoppers and souvenirs here.

Hidden amid a street full of European restaurants and dwarfed by the nearby St. Joseph's Cathedral, Japanese brand Nagu (20 Nha Tho, tel. 04/3928-8020, www.zan-toc.com, 9am-8pm daily) offers a combination of simple, understated women's clothing, accessories, homewares, and kids' toys with a local touch.

The vision of a French-Vietnamese designer, Marie-linh (74 Hang Trong, tel. 04/3928-6304, www.marie-linh.com, 9am-8pm daily) creates smart and affordable women's clothing. Combining high-quality fabrics with Eastern and Western influences, the shop's shirts, pants, shorts, and dresses offer casual comfort without sacrificing style.

A more upscale version of Marie-linh is open a few doors down, as is another location (11 Nha Tho, tel. 04/3928-8773, 9am-8pm daily) nearby.

A color-coded boutique that boasts "Western sizes at Vietnamese prices," Things of Substance (5 Nha Tho, tel. 04/3828-6965, www.prieure.com.vn, 9am-9pm daily) features women's wear with vibrant tops and flowing cotton and jersey dresses. There are few fitted items here, but the flowy styles are ideal for traveling and work well in the heat. Western-sized pants and a range of funky jewelry round out the shop's offerings.

In the wide, shallow storefront at Marena Hanoi (28 Nha Chung, tel. 04/3828-5542, www.marenahanoi.vn, 9am-6pm daily) there is barely enough room to turn around. Its shelves are packed with elegant, well-made ceramics and lacquerware, with much of its stock sticking to traditional themes. Simple blue-and-white designs adorn plates, tea sets, mugs, and small bowls, while lacquer trays and boxes boast brilliant reds or blacks. All items are handmade and prices are reasonable.

Ba Dinh District

Though this district is reserved more for historical sights than retail outlets, the one or two shops you'll find in Ba Dinh District are well worth your time.

54 Traditions (30 Hang Bun, tel. 04/3715-1569, www.54traditions.vn, 8am-6pm daily) celebrates the diverse cultures of Vietnam's 54 ethnicities, particularly its northern minority groups. Founded in 2004, the shop not only sells ancient artifacts, shamanic artwork, textiles, jewelry, and everyday objects of minority people, but also educates its customers on these items. Each purchase comes with at least 1,000 words of information on the object. Some stock dates all the way back to the Dong Son culture, and many items are museum-grade quality. Items range from a few dollars to a few thousand dollars.

Avid readers will be at home among the stacks of Bookworm (44 Chau Long, tel. 04/3715-3711, www.bookwormhanoi.com,

Tailor Made

Along Hang Gai and throughout the Old Quarter, tailors are easy to come by but quality and affordability together can be hard to find. A handful of standouts offer reliable service and skill at reasonable prices. Those who wish to have any tailoring done in Hanoi should plan ahead, as tailors in the capital tend to require more time than the speedy seamstresses of Hoi An. The average purchase can take anywhere from a few days to a week to complete, not including extra fittings or alterations. Most Hanoian tailors stock their own fabrics, saving you the trouble of visiting the market, though be prepared to pay a premium for this service. Whether you opt for the materials in-store or choose to purchase your own, it's best to swing by your preferred shop ahead of time to ensure that you buy enough of the required fabric and to get an idea of how much you should be paying for it.

Tagilis (12 Hang Bong, tel. 04/3990-7088, www.tagilis.wordpress.com, 9am-9pm daily) in the Old Quarter is your best bet for reasonably priced women's clothing. For a bit more quality try Ha Dong Silk (102 Hang Gai, tel. 04/3928-5056, hadongsilks@gmail.com, 8am-8pm daily), located on the same Old Quarter street, which provides a more upmarket range of fabrics and services. If it's more sophisticated tailoring you seek, West Lake shops like Clom's Closet (31A Xuan Dieu, tel. 04/3718-8233, cloclo@suit-ya.com, 9am-8pm daily), which takes orders on anything from men's and women's clothing to kidswear and even home linens, and the high-fashion Chula (6 Ven Ho Tay, tel. 09/0425-8960, www.chulafashion.com, 9am-6:30pm daily) come at a price but their quality is unmatched. Finally, men looking for affordable, well-made dress shirts and pants would do well to check out Zed's Threads (51A To Ngoc Van, tel. 09/4753-6515, www.zedsthreads.com, 10am-6pm daily), a men's-only tailoring shop also located in West Lake.

9am-7pm daily), an independent English-language bookstore. The shop boasts over 15,000 new and used titles in its two-story collection. A smaller room dedicated to Southeast Asia and Vietnam touches on topics such as history, culture, and local issues.

West Lake

For a calmer shopping experience, the West Lake neighborhood is home to more upmarket shopping, falling somewhere in between the Old Quarter and Trang Tien. Though it's less accessible than its southern counterparts, with shops fewer and farther between, the neighborhood includes a unique set of tailors for both men and women, not to mention a greater chance of finding Western sizes than Hanoi's downtown shops.

A small, colorful shop, To He (70 To Ngoc Van, tel. 04/3775-4230, www.tohe.vn, 8am-7pm daily) was borne out of a community program aimed at turning disadvantaged Vietnamese children on to their own creativity. The shop runs arts-related activities for kids with disabilities or serious illnesses, as well as those in orphanages, and uses the artwork and inspiration provided by its participants to create lovely printed bags, notebooks, table runners, T-shirts, and other souvenirs, whose proceeds go toward the continuation of the program.

Full of vivid colors and daring designs, the handmade dresses at Chula (6 Ven Ho Tay, tel. 09/0425-8960, www.chulafashion.com, 9am-6:30pm daily) are sure to get you noticed. The brainchild of a Spanish duo, this independent design house specializes in formal wear, creating vibrant, original pieces and tailor-made items for women. A wide array of ready-made outfits are available for purchase. You can also commission the skilled Diego to fashion something custom. Prices are similar to American department stores, but the quality is unparalleled.

Stepping into Clom's Closet (31A Xuan Dieu, tel. 04/3718-8233, cloclo@suit-ya.com, 9am-8pm daily) feels like entering a very fashionable wardrobe. Tastefully decorated and featuring men's and women's clothing, handbags, and accessories, this upmarket tailor produces truly beautiful formal wear using high-quality materials from around the world. Western prices apply here, but the quality and skill of Clom's tailors is well worth the cost.

While its fashion may not be as bold as other shops, Zed's Threads (51A To Ngoc Van, tel. 09/4753-6515, www.zedsthreads.com, 10am-6pm daily) is one of the only menswear stores in Hanoi that offers strictly men's clothing in sizes that fit Westerners. A range of quality shirts, pants, and suits take up the shop's racks. Made-to-measure services (8am-noon and 1pm-5pm Mon.-Sat.) are available, free of charge, though you'll have to make an appointment beforehand, either by phone or online.

Packed with plush quilts and bright home furnishings, Mekong Creations (58 Hang Trong, tel. 04/3824-4607, www.mekong-creations.org, 9am-9pm daily) offers well-made products for a good cause. Aimed at providing women in southern Vietnam and Cambodia with a sustainable income, this nonprofit organization has been assisting local communities since 2001. An array of quilts, bamboo products, and other housewares feature in this tiny shop, with half of the proceeds from each sale going back to the village from which the product came. For more variety, swing by Mekong Quilts (13 Hang Bac, tel. 04/3926-4831, www.mekong-quilts.org, 9am-9pm daily) nearby.

Sports and Recreation

There are a few activities for recreation once you've exhausted your sightseeing and shopping options. You'll find charming green spaces around the city. Spas are a growing industry, as are cooking classes, for those keen to master the art of Vietnamese cuisine.

PARKS

Scattered throughout Ba Dinh, Hoan Kiem, and Hai Ba Trung districts are Hanoi's array of small but well-loved parks, which serve as exercise tracks for early-risers, meeting spots for midday revelers, and communal areas for friends and family once the workday adjourns. While few of these green spaces could rival the parks you might find at home in terms of size, Hanoi's dozens of miniature clearings are a pleasant break from the madness of its usual hustle and bustle. The ring around Hoan Kiem Lake is the most popular of these areas, drawing hundreds of locals and tourists each day, including a small but devoted collection of young Vietnamese students hoping to strike up a conversation with a passing foreigner to practice their English.

Opposite Hoan Kiem Lake sits Ly Thai To Park (Dinh Tien Hoang between Le Lai and Le Thach), a modest square dominated by its imposing statue of the emperor of the same name. As the founder of Thang Long (what's now known as Hanoi), Ly Thai To features heavily on street signs, businesses, and monuments throughout Hanoi The open concrete square is packed with early-morning exercisers or rollerblading school kids later in the day.

A small wedge of green opposite the Military History Museum, Lenin Park (Dien Bien Phu between Hoang Dieu and Nguyen Tri Phuong) bears a domineering stone statue of its namesake at the far end of the clearing overlooking the city's famous Flag Tower. Trees line the edge of the concrete space, acting as a buffer between the downtown traffic and the relative peace of the square.

For a genuine escape from the Old Quarter chaos, Hanoi's Botanical Garden (Vuon Bach Thao, Hoang Hoa Tham, 7am-10pm daily, VND2,000) offers some much-appreciated silence in a city where noise pollution can wear on a person. In truth, this peaceful green space is pretty average, but thanks to its location and size, the pleasant grounds, equipped with two fish ponds, plenty of seating, and a collection of blocky, abstract sculptures, take the edge off Hanoi's frantic traffic. Animal-lovers would do well to bypass the cage near the entrance, as the birds inside are not particularly well looked after. While the park is a lovely place during the day, it's wise to stay away after dark, as this is a frequent hangout for some of Hanoi's more unsavory characters.

AMUSEMENT PARKS

One of Vincom's two mega malls, Royal City (72A Nguyen Trai, tel. 04/6276-7799, www.vincomshoppingmall.com, 9:30am-10pm daily) goes above and beyond your average retail center with an indoor waterfall, movie theater, bowling alley, arcade, water park, and Vietnam's one and only ice skating rink. Entry to the mall is free of charge, but use of the facilities costs money (from VND50,000 for a round of bowling; VND150,000 for access to the rink; VND170,000 for use of the water park). Vincom offers full-day "tours" of the shopping mall, hitting all of Royal City's major sights.

CYCLING

On the bicycle front, Hanoi has come a long way in recent years, cultivating a healthy crop of both local and expat cyclists who have taken to its streets in style, pedaling everything from flashy fixies to sleek, ultra-light road bikes to vintage, basket-toting city vehicles. Several small cycling communities exist throughout the city, meeting up for a jaunt down one of the larger roads or around West Lake. The capital has encountered some growing pains recently, as it attempts to make Hanoi a more bicycle-friendly city without altering the breakneck, chaotic traffic that congests its downtown streets. Bicycle rentals are possible and guided tours can be found through the city's best-known foreign cycling community, The Hanoi Bicycle Collective.

For cycling enthusiasts, a visit to The Hanoi Bicycle Collective (44 Ngo 31 Xuan Dieu, tel. 04/3718-8246, www.thbc.vn, 9am-6pm Mon.-Fri., 9am-7pm Sat.-Sun.) is a must. Founded in 2009 by Spaniard Guim

Valls Tereul and his Vietnamese wife Thuy Anh Nguyen, the shop has served as a base for Hanoi's foreign cycling community, offering bicycles and cycling gear for sale, city tours for curious travelers, and a regular "bike doctor" (Mon.-Sat.) to assist with repairs, as well as a small café (VND50,000-150,000) space. Peruse the upstairs display of goods or kick back on the ground floor with some Spanish tapas. A bulletin board along the café wall boasts a collection of foreign "cyclotourists" who have passed through THBC while traveling around the world on two wheels; the shop offers a complimentary maintenance check to those cycling through Hanoi. The shop runs regular tours (VND735,000) of downtown Hanoi and the West Lake area.

SWIMMING

Summertime temperatures in the city can be unforgiving, and one of the better ways to beat the heat is with a trip to the pool. A handful of high-end hotels allow pool access to non-guests, but day passes verge on exorbitant. The venues in this section are a more attractive option for those on a budget.

Overlooking scenic West Lake, the pool at Thang Loi Resort (200 Yen Phu, tel. 04/3829-4211 ext. 374, www.thangloihotel.vn, 6am-6pm daily, VND80,000) stays open year-round and offers changing rooms, lounge chairs, and access to the resort's restaurant and bar services. Though the pool is small, its location makes for a pleasant escape from the city's noise and affords nice views of the surrounding area. Bring your own towel, as these are not provided. The place gets crowded on weekends, usually in the afternoons, as local families bring their children for a swim.

Hanoi's only saltwater swimming venue, the Army Guesthouse Pool (33C Pham Ngu Lao, tel. 04/3825-2896, armyhotel@fpt.vn, 6:30am-9pm daily, VND90,000) escapes much of the downtown chaos, hiding at the end of a quiet, tree-lined avenue behind the Opera House. The lanes are large, and plenty of free space allows serious swimmers the opportunity to get some laps in. This spot is best avoided on weekends, namely in the afternoons, as families often turn up for downtime at the pool.

MASSAGES AND SPAS

While Hanoi boasts its fair share of quality massage parlors, spa services in the capital are more expensive than other destinations in the country. Tipping 15-20 percent is a standard practice in most massage parlors.

Aimed at training disadvantaged local youth for a career in massage therapy, Just Massage (237 Au Co, tel. 04/3718-2737, www.justmassage.org.vn, 9am-9pm daily, VND250,000-700,000) offers everything from Swedish and shiatsu massages to hot stones and aromatherapy treatments. Staff are friendly and speak English, allowing you to communicate with your massage therapist, and prices won't break the bank.

The tranquil SF Spa (30 Cua Dong, tel. 04/3747-5301, www.sfcompany.net, 9am-11:30pm daily, VND250,000-990,000), located on the western edge of the Old Quarter, is among Hanoi's more ambient retreats. Featuring a variety of foot and full-body massages, body treatments, facials, waxing, and all-encompassing spa packages, this charming day spa boasts a chic, simple modern decor along with experienced, English-speaking massage therapists.

Located within the Elegance Diamond Hotel on the eastern edge of the Old Quarter, La Siesta Spa (32 Lo Su, tel. 04/3935-1632, www.hanoielegancehotel.com, 8:30am-9pm daily, VND380,000-1,280,000) is a closer version of its swank home base, Zen Spa (100 Xuan Dieu, tel. 04/3719-1266, www.zenspa.com.vn, 9am-9pm daily, VNDVND380,000-1,280,000), out in West Lake. Boasting the same range of high-quality spa services, massages, facials, and body scrubs, the company's downtown facility provides a tranquil escape from the chaos outdoors, as well as several package treatments inspired by the principle of the five elements: earth, water, fire, metal, and wood.

COOKING CLASSES

Right in the heart of the Old Quarter, the Blue Butterfly (61 Hang Buom, tel. 04/3926-3845, www.bluebutterflyrestaurant.com, 9am and 3pm daily, VND735,000) runs half-day cooking classes every morning and afternoon. Three-hour courses begin with a trip to Dong Xuan Market, where a local chef will explain the finer points of Vietnamese produce before participants head back to the restaurant, don a chef's hat and apron, and begin to cook. Three basic but delicious local dishes feature on the class menu, all of which are included in the recipe book presented at the end of the session. Classes are small with up to 10 or 12 per group. This is a fun and different way for novice chefs to learn about local culture.

Boasting a range of courses designed by Australian chef Tracey Lister, co-author of three books on Vietnamese cuisine, the Hanoi Cooking Center (44 Chau Long, tel. 04/3715-0088, www.hanoicookingcentre.com, 9am-5:30pm daily, VND1,245,000) may offer the most expensive cooking classes in the city, but its experienced staff provide a clean environment, top-of-the-line cookware, and plenty of hands-on instruction about Vietnamese cuisine. Choose from several different themed courses, including a vegan tofu option, a session on barbecue and salads, and a half-day class devoted to spring rolls. Each course runs around four hours, with three in the kitchen and one to enjoy your sumptuous creations, and class sizes average 8-10 people. The center also offers street eats and market tours (Mon.-Sat., VND1,245,000), which take visitors on a four-hour trip around town, enjoying several varieties of local fare. Their Kids Club (VND320,000) allows children to partake in some basic, supervised cooking. Hanoi Cooking Center runs a small café (9am-5:30pm daily, VND70,000-140,000) space on the ground floor, serving mostly Western meals as well as European and Vietnamese coffee.

Accommodations

The bustling streets and narrow, snaking alleys of Hanoi's downtown districts hold accommodations to fit every budget, from basic dorm beds to palatial five-star suites. Base yourself within reach of Hoan Kiem Lake, as this will ensure a reasonable proximity to most of Hanoi's sights, restaurants, and shopping. With a reputation as one of the country's most walkable metropolises and a surplus of quality budget, mid-range, and high-end accommodations, there is no reason not to stay in the downtown area.

As travelers to the city will quickly learn, the Old Quarter is not a place for light sleepers. While there is no shortage of accommodations in Hanoi, several factors come into play when booking a room, not the least of which is noise level. Those with a tolerance for white noise or, at the very least, a set of earplugs will find no fault in the many rooms north of the lake; those who prefer more quiet may find peace down the web of alleys beside St. Joseph's Cathedral, where many of the cheaper budget accommodations have set up shop. A clutch of luxury hotels populates the French Quarter, many of them bearing unique historical significance in addition to high-end amenities and five-star service.

OLD QUARTER

This small but incredibly dense neighborhood manages to squeeze plenty of top-notch accommodations into a few blocks north of Hoan Kiem Lake, right in the center of the action. Prices run higher here while room sizes can be on the small side. Noise levels are higher than you might find elsewhere in the city.

Under VND210,000

Away from the spirited backpacker haunts, Hanoi Hostel (91C Hang Ma, tel. 04/6270-0006, www.vietnam-hostel.com, VND105,000 dorm) offers a peaceful place for weary budget travelers to lay their heads. The mixed and female dorms have clean, comfy beds and en suite bathrooms, personal lockers, daily breakfast, and a free happy-hour beer. The outfit in charge runs a tour service downstairs. While there's not really much of a common area, this hostel's location and laid-back vibe make up for that. There is also a second location (32 Hang Vai, tel. 04/6270-2009) nearby.

Hanoi Backpackers' Downtown (9 Ma May, tel. 04/3935-1890, www.vietnam-backpackerhostels.com, VND158,000 dorm, VND973,000 double) is a good option for those in search of travel buddies, though if it's quiet you seek, then this is not the place to crash. Single mixed dorms, female-only rooms, and double bed dorms are available, all with personal lockers, air-conditioning, Wi-Fi, and communal bathrooms. Breakfast is served in the restaurant each morning. Though a few private rooms are available, you're better off going elsewhere if you'd prefer your own space.

VND210,000-525,000

The Tu Linh Palace 2 (86 Ma May, tel. 04/3826-9999, www.tulinhpalacehotel.com, VND462,000-588,000, breakfast included) is run by a welcoming and attentive staff and, for the price, offers decent value. Standard amenities such as hot water, air-conditioning, TV, and Wi-Fi access are available. A bar and restaurant on the ground floor round out Tu Linh's offerings.

Rooms at Hanoi City Hostel (95B Hang Ga, tel. 04/3828-1379, www.hanoicityhostel.com, VND336,000-378,000, breakfast included) are spacious and a bit worn but right for the price, counting hot water, air-conditioning, TV, Wi-Fi, a fridge, and tea- and coffee-making facilities among its standard amenities. Both front- and back-facing rooms are available, the former boasting large windows and lots of light, the latter offering more quiet away from the traffic noise of the downtown area. The staff can help arrange onward travel and transportation.

VND525,000-1,050,000

Though rooms at the Rising Dragon Legend (55 Hang Be, tel. 04/3935-2647, www.risingdragonhotel.com, VND525,000-1,470,000, breakfast included) are decidedly small, this skinny budget venture offers decent value for money, with clean, modern furnishings and comfy beds, hot water, air-conditioning, TV, minibar, in-room safe, Wi-Fi access, and tea- and coffee-making facilities. The hotel staff are a friendly and professional bunch who assist with travel bookings around northern Vietnam.

In a big and hectic city, the Hanoi Guesthouse (85 Ma May, tel. 04/3935-2572, www.hanoiguesthouse.com, VND525,000-840,000, breakfast included) truly feels like a homier stay than most, with free refreshments on tap in the lobby and a notably attentive staff. Rooms are a great value, outfitted with TV, Wi-Fi, hot water, air-conditioning, a minibar, an in-room safe, and tea- and coffee-making facilities. Add-ons include airport transfer, travel bookings, laundry, and luggage storage.

Cozy, well-appointed, and right in the heart of the Old Quarter, rooms at the Hanoi Old Town (95 Hang Chieu, tel. 04/3929-0783, www.hanoioldtown.com, VND525,000-840,000, breakfast included) feature generously sized beds, hot water, television, air-conditioning, and Wi-Fi access. Facilities are older than other hotels in the area, but staff at the Old Town are a cheerful bunch and assist with travel services and tours around northern Vietnam. For lots of light and a street view, front-facing rooms are a solid choice; but if you prefer peace and quiet, opt for a spot at the back, where noise levels aren't so high.

Rooms at the Hanoi Paradise Hotel (53 Hang Chieu, tel. 04/3929-0026, www.hanoiparadisehotel.com, VND735,000-1,680,000)

are smart, cozy, and outfitted with some unusual amenities, including in-room computers that would not be out of place in an antiques museum. Other amenities include air-conditioning, hot water, TV, Wi-Fi, and tea- and coffee-making facilities. Staff are friendly and exceptionally service-minded, taking this mid-range accommodation above and beyond the rest. Both street- and back-facing rooms are available, depending upon your tolerance for city noise levels.

★ Golden Time Hostel 2 (8 Ly Thai To, tel. 04/3825-9654, www.goldentimehostel.com, VND420,000-945,000, breakfast included) is not a hostel but a budget hotel. Its location east of Hoan Kiem Lake affords travelers the best of both worlds: beyond the bustle and noise of the Old Quarter and yet close to the city center. Rooms are well-kept and come with television, air-conditioning, hot water, Wi-Fi access, and an in-room safe. Some rooms don't have windows. The staff is attentive and assists with transportation and travel bookings. For a slightly cheaper but equally worthy option, Golden Time 1 (43 Ly Thai To, tel. 04/3935-1091, www.goldentimehostel.com, VND294,000-378,000) is just down the road. While there's less atmosphere here, good service and most of the same amenities apply.

VND1,050,000-2,100,000

Hugging the western edge of the Old Quarter, the Charming Hotel 2 (31 Hang Ga, tel. 04/3923-4031, www.hanoicharminghotel.com, VND945,000-1,890,000, breakfast included) provides five-star service for a fraction of the price. Rooms are modern and well-appointed, with in-room amenities such as a computer, safe, work desk, TV, and Wi-Fi access, as well as complimentary water and tea- and coffee-making facilities. The hotel offers a handful of different room types, from standard superiors, with and without windows, to spacious executive accommodations.

The 25-room Oriental Central Hotel (39 Hang Bac, tel. 04/3935-1117, www.orientalcentralhotel.com, VND945,000-1,575,000, breakfast included) stands out thanks to top-notch staff and a modern look. Well-appointed rooms come with the standard amenities as well as complimentary daily water. The antique-style bronze showerheads and framed photographs of everyday Vietnamese scenes add to the ambience. The superior, deluxe, and suite rooms have varying degrees of natural light. Opt for at least a deluxe, as these afford a better view. Additional services like travel bookings and airport pickup can be arranged.

Calypso Suites Hotel (11E Trung Yen, Dinh Liet, tel. 04/3935-2751, www.calypso-suiteshotel.com, VND840,000-1,575,000, breakfast included), run by the same people as Oriental Central Hotel, bears a similar red, black, and white design scheme and equally conscientious service. Expect standard amenities as well as Wi-Fi, DVD players, and in-room safes. The hotel's alley location minimizes the noise of the Old Quarter.

The Essence Hanoi Hotel (22 Ta Hien, tel. 04/3935-2485, www.essencehanoihotel.com, VND1,365,000-2,415,000, breakfast included) provides quality service and posh, mid-range boutique rooms that feature in-room computers, in-room safes, and daily complimentary water on top of the standard amenities. The hotel's restaurant operates throughout the day on an à la carte menu. Services such as laundry, luggage storage, and tour bookings can be arranged at reception. Rooms vary in size and access to natural light; take a step up from the most basic option for a room with a view.

Part of the Elegance chain, Hanoi Elegance Diamond Hotel (32 Lo Su, tel. 04/3935-1632, www.hanoielegancehotel.com, VND1,260,000-2,310,000) is one of the company's best properties. Perched on the edge of the Old Quarter, the Diamond houses boutique rooms and the Gourmet Corner, a much-touted top-floor restaurant with pleasant lake views, as well as an outdoor terrace bar. Rooms feature a simple but elegant decor, plush beds, an in-room safe, computer, and complimentary water alongside the usual amenities.

The grand Tirant Hotel (36-38 Gia Ngu, tel. 04/6269-8899, www.tiranthotel.com,

VND1,575,000-3,045,000) boasts a larger property than much of its Old Quarter competition, no easy feat in this packed neighborhood. Above the lavish reception area, 63 well-appointed rooms are outfitted in regal furnishings and come with an in-room computer, minibar, and tea- and coffee-making facilities in addition to standard hotel amenities. Breakfast is served in the hotel's downstairs restaurant each morning. A lake-view lounge tops the building, affording pleasant views of Hoan Kiem Lake. You'll find a fitness center and a small swimming pool here, as well as a travel desk, which assists with transportation and tour bookings.

CATHEDRAL DISTRICT

Situated just north of St. Joseph's Cathedral is a tiny backpacker enclave on Ngo Huyen that provides decent rooms at lower prices than in the Old Quarter.

Under VND210,000

The original Hanoi Backpackers' (48 Ngo Huyen, tel. 04/3828-5372, www.vietnam-backpackerhostels.com, VND158,000 dorm, VND680,000 double, breakfast included) sits about halfway down narrow Ngo Huyen, a stone's throw from the Cathedral and Hoan Kiem Lake. Both mixed and all-female beds are available, with hot water, Wi-Fi, air-conditioning, and personal lockers. While there are a handful of private rooms, it's better to look elsewhere for quiet, because the crowd here likes to party. The staff can help arrange onward travel and transportation.

It's a little less tidy than Hanoi Backpackers', but Central Backpackers (16 Ly Quoc Su, tel. 04/3938-1849, www.central-backpackershostel.com, VND105,000 dorm, VND462,000 double, breakfast included) is an affordable option. Mixed dorms are outfitted with personal lockers, air-conditioning, and Wi-Fi, with hot water in the shared bathrooms. During happy hour, you can enjoy a daily free beer. This is a good backpacker spot. The private rooms are not worthwhile; for peace and quiet, look elsewhere.

VND210,000-525,000

Especen Hotel (28 Tho Xuong, tel. 04/3824-4401, www.especen.vn, VND336,000-525,000) offers clean, spacious rooms in the heart of the Cathedral District. Tucked down an alley, the hotel is a five-minute walk from Hoan Kiem Lake. Rooms offer single- or queen-size beds and come equipped with a television, air-conditioning, Wi-Fi, and hot water. Long-term stays can be arranged for a discounted rate, and the friendly hotel staff can assist with travel plans around the city as well as throughout the north. There are a number of copycats in the area that have duplicated the hotel's sign. Go to this exact address to avoid impostors.

The Bluebell Hotel (41 Ngo Huyen, tel. 04/3938-2398, www.hanoibluebellhotel.com, VND420,000-630,000), hidden among the clutch of budget accommodations beside the cathedral, is one of this alley's better options, offering clean and well-priced rooms kitted out with hot water, air-conditioning, tea- and coffee-making facilities, fridge, TV, and Wi-Fi. If you're willing to hike up a few flights of stairs, the higher floors are better, as they tend to minimize the noise. All rooms are well-appointed and the friendly staff can assist with travel bookings and transportation.

In the shadow of St. Joseph's, the Rising Dragon Cathedral (38 Au Trieu, tel. 04/3826-8500, www.risingdragonhotel.com, VND462,000-1,575,000, breakfast included) offers great value for the money. Its charming, well-kept accommodations come with not only the standard hotel amenities, from hot water and air-conditioning to television and Wi-Fi access, but also a generous window and private balcony for each room. The balcony is the perfect spot to take in the morning bustle of the neighborhood or wind down after a long day. The unlimited refreshments downstairs are complimentary.

Tucked tightly down an alley off the road circling Hoan Kiem Lake, Little Hanoi Hostel 2 (32 Le Thai To, tel. 04/3928-9897, www.littlehanoihostel.com, VND462,000 double, breakfast included) is a pleasant surprise. Quaint, quiet, and incredibly close to the water, this mini-hotel's location eliminates much of the noise problem that comes with being downtown. It boasts cozy, well-kept accommodations that count air-conditioning, hot water, Wi-Fi access, TV, and natural light among their amenities. The staff are a cheerful bunch, willing to help with transportation and travel arrangements, as well as city recommendations.

Though it's a little aged, Tung Trang (13 Tam Thuong, tel. 04/3828-6267, tungtrang-hotel@yahoo.com, VND315,000-546,000) stands out for its peaceful location, nestled amid a tangle of alleys just off Hang Bong. Rooms are basic, featuring hot water, air-conditioning, TV, and Wi-Fi access, all complimented nicely by the hospitality of the staff. Front rooms are spacious and include balconies, while smaller, cheaper accommodations are also available.

VND525,000-1,050,000

The most affordable in a chain of well-run, family-owned accommodations, Splendid Jupiter Hotel (16 Tho Xuong, tel. 04/3938-1831, www.splendidstarhotel.com, VND525,000-945,000, breakfast included) features bright, comfortable rooms with hot water, air-conditioning, TV, Wi-Fi access, complimentary water, an in-room safe, mini-bar, tea- and coffee-making facilities, and a DVD player. The staff can help arrange onward travel and transportation.

Decked out in miniature chandeliers, plush carpet, and snakeskin wallpaper, the Angel Palace Hotel (173 Hang Bong, tel. 04/6299-8666, www.angelpalacehotel.com.vn, VND945,000-1,470,000, breakfast included) makes a statement with its style as well as its service. All accommodations are modern and well-appointed, counting hot water, air-conditioning, TV, Wi-Fi access, complimentary water, a writing desk, and tea- and coffee-making facilities in the standard list of amenities. Additional services, such as laundry and tour arrangements, can be made with the friendly and professional folks at the front desk.

The smart and service-minded Aranya Hotel (128 Hang Bong, tel. 04/3938-2250, www.aranyahotel.com, VND945,000-1,785,000, breakfast included) hovers on the western edge of the Old Quarter. Outfitted with 30 guest rooms, each accommodation features air-conditioning, hot water, television, Wi-Fi access, complimentary water, and tea- and coffee-making facilities. The Aranya also counts a restaurant, spa, and travel services in its offerings.

VND1,050,000-2,100,000

Tried and trusted, the Hanoi City Palace Hotel (106 Hang Bong, tel. 04/3938-2333, www.hanoicitypalacehotel.com, VND1,155,000-2,100,000, breakfast included) boasts top-notch service and a chic decor that exceeds the level of most mid-range accommodations. Rooms at this charming boutique hotel feature spacious bathrooms as well as a work desk, minibar, television, in-room safe, tea- and coffee-making facilities, and complimentary water. Suite rooms include a private balcony. Additional touches like a welcome drink and fruit platter highlight the staff's attention to detail. The hotel runs a travel desk, which assists with tours around the city and beyond.

FRENCH QUARTER

The chic French Quarter is home to the city's most historic and high-end hotels. From the world-famous Metropole to elegant modern hotels like Nikko, Hotel de l'Opera, and Hanoi Hilton Opera, this is a neighborhood for the more affluent traveler.

Over VND2,100,000

The spectacular, stately Sofitel Legend Metropole (15 Ngo Quyen, tel. 04/3826-6919, www.sofitel.com, VND5,565,000-46,095,000) opened in 1901. Its historic white building, with black shutters and stocky balustrades, earned a reputation as the finest hotel in Indochina, catering to famous visitors and well-to-do residents. The five-star opulence of the Metropole is evident in its plush, sophisticated rooms, which come with a television and complimentary bottled water. The hotel boasts a pair of luxurious restaurants, a spa, swimming pool, gift shop, sauna, and fitness center.

The five-star Hanoi Hilton Opera (1 Le Thanh Tong, tel. 04/3933-0500, www3.hilton.com, VND3,255,000-22,155,000) stands just south of the city's historic theater and exudes class from its regal, vaulted reception hall all the way to the elegant, well-appointed guest rooms. Accommodations feature standard hotel amenities alongside a minibar, in-room safe, Internet access, and tea- and coffee-making facilities. A fitness center, outdoor pool, sports bar, two restaurants, and a swanky café round out the hotel's offerings.

An imposing white building, the plush Nikko Hotel (84 Tran Nhan Tong, tel. 04/3822-3535, www.hotelnikkohanoi.com.vn, VND2,310,000-12,495,000, breakfast included) boasts 257 guest rooms, ranging from deluxe rooms to park view and executive lodgings and suites. Outfitted with high-quality amenities such as television, Wi-Fi access, a spacious bathroom, and a small sitting alcove, all rooms are well-appointed and come with use of the hotel swimming pool, whirlpool tub, and fitness center. The Nikko counts a spa, a bar, and three restaurants in its offerings.

A cross between cozy guesthouse and high-end hotel, the Hilton Garden Inn (20 Phan Chu Trinh, tel. 04/3944-9396, www.hiltongardeninn3.hilton.com, VND1,995,000-4,200,000) provides a more casual approach to luxury accommodation, with B&B-style lodgings alongside five-star service. Room amenities include television, Wi-Fi access, an in-room safe, desk, refrigerator, and tea- and coffee-making facilities, as well as use of the business center and gym. A bar, restaurant, and 24-hour pantry market round out the inn's additional services.

The Hotel de l'Opera (29 Trang Tien, tel. 04/6282-5555, www.mgallery.com, VND3,150,000-6,300,000) is not the first five-star hotel to grace this spot. At the turn of the 20th century, an elegant building known as the Hanoi Hotel served as a popular meeting place for local socialites. That building was eventually torn down in 2004 and rebuilt. Now outfitted with bold decor and first-class facilities, including flat-screen television and Wi-Fi access, the hotel stands out for its unique design, furnished in vivid, eye-catching colors. The chic, ground-floor Cafe Lautrec is a posh and popular French Quarter dining spot.

Tucked between high-rise office buildings and sprawling department stores, the De Syloia (17A Tran Hung Dao, tel. 04/3824-5346, www.desyloia.com, VND2,100,000-2,730,000, breakfast included) is a cozy boutique hotel modeled after a colonial-style villa. Each well-appointed room comes with Wi-Fi access, TV, an in-room safe, minibar, and complimentary water. Guests have access to the hotel's gym and business center. De Syloia's restaurant, Cay Cau, features both Vietnamese cuisine and live traditional music nightly from 7pm.

WEST LAKE

West Lake, with a handful of secluded high-end hotels, is the quietest neighborhood in the capital city. Xuan Dieu, the street bordering the eastern edge of the water, features several nice restaurants and bars, though options are limited.

Over VND2,100,000

Well removed from the chaos of downtown, the Sheraton Hanoi (11 Xuan Dieu, tel. 04/3719-9000, www.sheratonhanoi.com, VND2,310,000-34,965,000) sits just over two miles from the Old Quarter and has a pool, spa, garden, opulent lobby, and several restaurants on its sprawling lake shore property. Guest rooms feature the standard hotel amenities as well as a minibar, fridge, in-room safe, complimentary water, and tea- and coffee-making facilities.

Off the eastern shore of the lake, Intercontinental West Lake (1A Nghi Tam, tel. 04/6270-8888, www.ihg.com, VND2,835,000-34,335,000) boasts over 300 guest rooms, including stunning over-water pavilions connected to the water's edge by a maze of floating walkways. Plush rooms are outfitted with a fusion of traditional Asian-inspired elements and modern decor, and include Wi-Fi access and a private balcony. The hotel's three restaurants serve a range of international and Vietnamese cuisine. The outdoor pool and a state-of-the-art fitness center are free for guests to use.

Nestled between West Lake and Truc Bach, the Sofitel Plaza Hanoi (1 Thanh Nien, tel. 04/3823-8888, www.sofitel.com, VND5,250,000-8,820,000) is blessed with attractive natural surroundings. The Sofitel's location brings travelers closer to the heart of the city while still providing peace and quiet. The five-star hotel boasts 273 guest rooms outfitted with plush modern decor, an in-room safe, Wi-Fi access, and a flat-screen television. A pair of posh restaurants showcase Chinese, Western, and Vietnamese cuisine, while the Summit Lounge overlooks the lake. A swimming pool, spa, and fitness center are part of the Sofitel's offerings.

Food

Holding the distinction of best pho in Vietnam, the capital city collectively enjoys thousands of helpings each morning. Other Hanoian specialties earn equal notoriety for their flavors and textures. The unsung hero is *bun cha,* a delicious northern version of grilled meat and rice noodles doused in *nuoc cham,* a diluted fish sauce that comes with pickled veggies, fresh greens, and the occasional fried spring roll. You'll find this mouthwatering specialty on every street corner and likely smell it from a few blocks away, as the scent of barbecue floats up from street stalls. What Hanoi does, it does well: Mouthwatering, square-shaped seafood spring rolls, also known as *nem cua be,* are a must-eat in the capital. Several *cha ca* (pan-fried fish) restaurants round out the best Vietnamese offerings.

Hanoi's non-Vietnamese fare offers plenty of variety, from Indian and Malaysian meals to Thai, French, and American. Upscale eateries make a greater effort in the service department, opting for a Western approach, and there are more than a few foreign chefs and owners behind some of the city's well-known Western restaurants. The need for reservations is greater here, as the limited space of the Old Quarter means that dining rooms fill up fast.

The streets of Hanoi are a good place to experience roadside dining in Vietnam. Crammed onto already-busy sidewalks and hidden down narrow alleys, chefs serve everything from tasty Vietnamese sandwiches to piping hot soups, rice porridge, barbecue, and local specialties, often at VND40,000 or less per meal.

Safe street food is easy to find, provided you stick to clean outdoor kitchens. When in doubt, look for hot meals, such as soups or grilled meats. High temperatures tend to eliminate some of the risk.

OLD QUARTER
Cafés and Bakeries

Modest and unassuming, Giang Cafe (39 Nguyen Huu Huan, www.giangcafehanoi. com, 7am-10pm daily, VND15,000-30,000), in business since 1946, is hidden from the street by a narrow passageway between two larger storefronts. Try a cup of Hanoi's famous *ca phe trung* (egg coffee). This may not sound appetizing, but the thick, decadent concoction is a treat on a cold day, a combination of egg yolks, condensed milk, and Vietnamese coffee. The modest shop serves regular coffee, tea, and other refreshments at local prices. Its founder, Nguyen Giang, worked as a bartender at the legendary Metropole hotel before opening Giang Cafe.

French-Vietnamese Fusion

One of Hanoi's best-known venues, Green Tangerine (48 Hang Be, tel. 04/3825-1286, www.greentangerinehanoi.com, 11am-11pm daily, VND175,000-600,000) specializes in French and Vietnamese fusion, pairing unlikely ingredients to create unique and memorable dishes. The restaurant's 1928 colonial villa makes a worthy setting for a fancy meal. Prices run high, but the set menus offer decent value, with two-course lunches beginning at VND218,000 and a three-course dinner going for VND499,000. Given its popularity (it has been featured in a handful of high-profile publications, as well as on CNN's Travel website), reservations are a good idea.

Gastropubs

A classy pub and grill, The Moose & Roo (42B Ma May, tel. 04/3200-1289, www.mooseandroo.com, 9:30am-midnight daily, VND120,000-500,000) serves hearty pub dishes, from burgers, steaks, and savory pies to full Western breakfasts. Beer, wine, and cocktails are on offer, including hard-to-find top-shelf scotches and whiskeys. Dining in this cozy narrow space is well worth the price, and it makes for an excellent spot to unwind after a day of shopping and sightseeing.

Indian

The best of Hanoi's clutch of Indian restaurants, Little India (23 Hang Tre, tel. 04/3926-1859, www.little-india-hn.com, 10:30am-2:30pm and 6pm-10:30pm daily, VND45,000-115,000) boasts not only an impressive range of Indian cuisine but also a list of Malaysian dishes, including *nasi goreng* and beef *rendang,* as well as a few Chinese meals. Portions are generous, prices are right, and the staff aim to please. As a 100-percent halal establishment, you won't find alcohol here, but you're no more than a few blocks from nightlife venues, should you require a nightcap afterward.

Street Food

A Hanoi institution, Xoi Yen (35B Nguyen Huu Huan, tel. 04/3934-1950, 6am-midnight daily, VND15,000-50,000) is always packed with locals. Specializing in savory *xoi* (sticky rice), this restaurant features a menu of assorted toppings, including meats such as *xa xiu,* also known as *char siu* (Chinese-style

roast pork), chicken, *cha* (a type of Vietnamese processed meat), or claypot-braised pork, which accompany your choice of sticky rice. Low tables and stools populate both the ground floor and the open-air second story. Visit the one on the corner and not its impostor next door.

Directly opposite Hang Da Market is a small, open-front shop that doles out tasty *mien luon* (87 Hang Dieu, tel. 04/3826-7943, 7am-10:30pm daily, VND20,000-50,000). The bowls of piping hot soup feature glass noodles and fried eel. Order the rice porridge or any of the other eel dishes from a large picture menu mounted on the wall. The metal-and-plastic furniture fit right in with the street-food vibe.

Fresh, flavorful, and good enough for seconds, the *bun bo nam bo* (67 Hang Dieu, 7:30am-10:30pm daily, VND55,000/bowl) at the skinny storefront near Hang Da Market is a popular choice among locals. Metal tables line the long, narrow dining area and a dexterous assembly line prepares heaping portions of the tasty rice noodle and beef dish, complete with fresh greens, pickled carrots, peanuts, and sauce.

While there are hundreds of street stalls serving this classic Hanoian dish, the ★ *bun cha* (34 Hang Than, tel. 04/3927-0879,

Local institution Xoi Yen stays busy from morning to night.

9am-2pm or until sold out daily, VND35,000/bowl) is the best of its kind. Hearty helpings of grilled pork and ground meat come swimming in *nuoc cham,* a lighter cousin of fish sauce, accompanied by pickled carrots and daikon. Add rice noodles and as many fresh greens as you'd like, stir, and enjoy. This spot only opens for lunch, and its product is well known among locals.

If you're short on time or prefer to stay closer to the Old Quarter, **Bun Cha Dac Kim** (1 Hang Manh, tel. 04/3828-7060, www.bunchahangmanh.vn, 10am-7pm daily, VND60,000/bowl) is another well-known local spot for *bun cha.* The owners overcharge foreigners, sometimes as much as VND90,000 for a meal.

Vietnamese

Even amid scores of backpacker eateries and shops catering to Western tourists, **New Day** (72 Ma May, tel. 04/3828-0315, www.newdayrestaurant.com, 10am-9pm daily, VND30,000-200,000) retains a strong local following. With a well-rounded menu that covers everything from pork, chicken, and beef to frog, duck, oysters, and vegetarian fare, New Day has reasonable prices.

Cha Ca La Vong (14 Cha Ca, tel. 04/3823-9875, 11am-2pm and 5:30pm-9pm daily, VND170,000/person) is the city's oldest restaurant, serving up sizzling pans of *cha ca* (pan-fried fish) since 1871. The modest, two-story spot specializes in only one dish, accompanied by rice noodles and peanuts. The portions are undersized and overpriced, though tasty. The staff is abrupt, but the restaurant is a popular stop. If you'd prefer more service and larger portions, **Cha Ca Thang Long** (21-31 Duong Thanh, tel. 04/3824-5115, www.chacathanglong.com, 10am-10pm daily, VND120,000/person) provides the same dish at a more reasonable price.

At the charming **Little Black Duck** (23 Ngo Gach, tel. 04/6253-5557, www.littleblackduckhanoi.com, 10:30am-10pm daily, VND50,000-380,000), Vietnamese cuisine is the main offering, though dishes like falafel

bun cha, a Hanoian noodle specialty

and fish and chips are on the menu. There are several duck specialties, including a tasty *bun nem vit* (soup with rice noodles, fresh greens, and duck spring rolls). The miniature eatery feels like a café, with only three tables in its ground-floor dining area and the rest occupying a cozy space upstairs. The staff is friendly and eager to please.

Com Ga (1 Cua Dong, tel. 04/3923-3728, comgacafe@gmail.com, 7am-11pm daily, VND55,000-135,000) sits on a busy corner along the western edge of the Old Quarter. The restaurant prides itself on its hearty helpings of the namesake *com ga* (Hoi An-style chicken and rice). The second-floor balcony makes an ideal spot for a drink and late-afternoon people-watching.

CATHEDRAL DISTRICT
Cafés and Bakeries

Seek out the pocket-sized **Hanoi House** (47A Ly Quoc Su, 2nd Fl., tel. 04/2348-9789, 8:30am-11pm daily, VND24,000-87,000) and you'll be rewarded with a cozy, laid-back hideout just far enough from the bustle of the city. All but invisible from the street, this tiny café is down an alley and up a flight of concrete stairs, overlooking St. Joseph's Cathedral. Furnished with low wooden tables and intimate booths, ceramic tea sets, small Chinese ink paintings, and rattan-weaved lanterns, Hanoi House offers the usual coffee and tea options in a pleasantly relaxed space.

A large, comfy, Western-style shop, **Joma Bakery & Cafe** (22 Ly Quoc Su, tel. 04/3747-3388, www.joma.biz, 7am-9pm daily, VND30,000-120,000) offers a taste of home, with delicious breakfasts, sandwiches, bagels, European coffee, and mouthwatering pastries. Relax in the small seating area up front near the main counter, or head out back to the larger café, where cozy couches and quiet tables await. You'll also find another location at **Joma To Ngoc Van** (43 To Ngoc Van, tel. 04/3718-6071, www.joma.biz, 7am-9pm daily, VND30,000-120,000). Both outlets have delivery services. A portion of their sales go to local charitable organizations.

Just off the main drag, the storefront of **Loft Stop Cafe** (11B Bao Khanh, tel. 04/3928-9433, www.loft-stop-cafe.com, 8am-11pm daily, VND25,000-200,000) is lit up by two well-stocked display cases laden with decadent treats. Pastries, cakes, and other goodies attract more than a few visitors. Its cool, quiet, street-side digs offer some respite, and with a range of coffee, tea, and other beverages populating the menu, it's a good place to pop in for dessert or a mid-afternoon snack. The Loft Stop also makes a solid pizza.

International

The **Hanoi Social Club** (6 Hoi Vu, tel. 04/3938-2117, 8am-11pm daily, VND95,000-170,000) dishes out an eclectic array of international fare, including burgers and breakfast foods alongside goulash, roti wraps, mango curry, and Moroccan chicken. Its chefs are able to adjust dishes for vegetarian, vegan, and gluten-free diners. The beverage menu is equally varied, including European coffees and teas as well as a few Vietnamese favorites,

such as egg coffee and *ca phe sua da* (iced coffee with milk). Comfy chairs, whimsical decor, and indie music round out the Social Club's offerings. There is live music on evenings and weekends.

It's hard not to be charmed by the laid-back ambience and breezy second-floor balcony at classy **Buon Dua Le Cafe** (20 Hang Hanh, tel. 04/3825-7388, 6:30am-11pm daily, VND45,000-275,000). Down a quiet side street but close to Hoan Kiem Lake, the place is outfitted with polished wooden furniture and the artwork of local painter Duc Loi. The menu is mainly Vietnamese, with a few Western dishes. The open-air hangout makes a perfect place to start your day or kick back with a happy hour beverage as the sun goes down.

Street Food

One bowl of rice porridge, called *chao suon* (corner of Ly Quoc Su and Ngo Huyen, 7am-7pm daily, VND25,000/bowl), from the small, street-side outfit near St. Joseph's Cathedral and you'll be coming back for seconds. A smooth, stew-like consistency, this particular vendor's porridge is served with savory pork and *quay,* essentially a fried breadstick, on top. On the miniature plastic stools that line the road, sit and enjoy the bustle of the city while tucking into your piping hot *chao.* For extra flavor, toss in some black pepper. Portions are just right, making this a great breakfast or midday snack.

Vietnamese

A top-seven contender on Vietnam's first-ever edition of *MasterChef,* the talented **Minh Thuy** (20 Ngo Huyen, tel. 04/3200-7893, www.minh-thuy.com, 10am-10pm daily, VND40,000-130,000) excels at preparing local dishes as well as her very own European-Asian fusions. Tucked down an alley flush with budget hotels and hungry travelers, the small, one-room restaurant has flourished as both locals and tourists stop in for a bite and a glimpse of the framed *MasterChef* apron. With great food and reasonable prices, this is a go-to spot for lunch and dinner.

FRENCH QUARTER
French

La Badiane (10 Nam Ngu, tel. 04/3942-4509, www.labadiane-hanoi.com, 11:30am-2:30pm and 6:30pm-10:30pm Mon.-Sat., VND230,000-345,000 lunch, VND520,000-1,590,000 dinner) is the city's finest French restaurant. Venture through the restaurant's arching, vine-covered white corridor and you'll find a host of gourmet dishes, from lamb shank and duck breast, tartar and carpaccio to pan-fried foie gras, homemade pasta, and sumptuous desserts. Each meal is a work of art, carefully plated. Chef Benjamin Rascalou, a veteran of the Parisian restaurant circuit, keeps things interesting with a regularly changing menu.

Thai

There is a consensus among locals and expats that Lustro Thai (57A Phan Chu Trinh, tel. 04/6278-2628, 9am-11pm daily, VND85,000-265,000) is the best Thai spot in the French Quarter. With generous helpings of authentic fare and a spacious, modern seating area, the restaurant earns its popularity.

Vegetarian

Hidden down an alley, Nang Tam Com Chay (79A Tran Hung Dao, tel. 04/3942-4140, 10am-9pm daily, VND25,000-100,000) is a popular Vietnamese vegetarian joint that features scores of meatless dishes, from standard tofu-and-tomato-sauce to mock-meat recreations of traditional local fare. Tasty, filling set lunches go for as little as VND60,000. The small, air-conditioned dining area is usually full of locals at both lunch and dinner.

Vietnamese

Ngon (18 Phan Boi Chau, tel. 04/3942-8162, www.ngonhanoi.com.vn, 6:30am-9:30pm daily, VND45,000-360,000) and its extensive menu provide solid guidance on what to eat and how to eat it. Thanks to the place's

market-style setup, diners are able to peruse everything before choosing. Set within a large courtyard, the bustling street food-style eatery is packed during lunch and evenings with tourists and locals. Delve into soups, sautés, spring rolls, and sauces.

BA DINH
Cafés and Bakeries

The folks at Cong Caphe (32 Dien Bien Phu, tel. 04/6686-0344, www.congcaphe.com, 7am-11pm daily, VND30,000-50,000) have taken the aesthetics of Vietnamese Communism and applied it to an urban coffee shop, with a decor featuring weathered wood, peeling paint, exposed brick, and stark concrete. The brown-paper menus list coffee, tea, and smoothies alongside coffee-coconut shakes and coffee with yogurt. There are other locations (35A Nguyen Huu Huan, tel. 04/6292-5814, 7am-11pm daily) around town, including a spot on Nguyen Huu Huan. Cong occasionally hosts live music, during which time it serves a few alcoholic beverages.

International

A training restaurant and one of the most popular spots in town, KOTO (59 Van Mieu, tel. 04/3747-0337, www.koto.com.au, 7:30am-10pm daily, VND85,000-250,000) has made an impact on the restaurant scene as well as the lives of its many graduates. Started in 1999, KOTO (Know One, Teach One) admits young disadvantaged Vietnamese into its two-year training program, which provides job training in the hospitality industry. The restaurant acts as a training ground for students while serving delicious renditions of both Vietnamese and international favorites. The eatery's location makes it conducive to a lunchtime visit, though things can get hectic around this time. Seating is spread out over four floors.

Many KOTO graduates have gone on to open their own restaurants, the most popular of which is Pots 'n Pans (57 Bui Thi Xuan, tel. 04/3944-0204, www.potsnpans.vn, 11:30am-late daily, VND210,000-690,000), an upmarket fusion spot with high-quality service and plenty of ambience. Though it's expensive, the food is truly a work of art; opt for one of the set menus, as these offer the best value.

Street Food

If you are near the Temple of Literature in the afternoon, swing by Ly Van Phuc, where you'll find finger-licking barbecue chicken (end of Ly Van Phuc, 4pm-late daily, VND6,000-10,000/piece) starting around 3pm-4pm. Snacks are pay-as-you-go, with varying prices for legs and wings. These tasty treats make the perfect *do nhau* (drinking food) to pair with a beer. Though there are several shops along this street, the ones at the far end are the best.

WEST LAKE AREA
Cafés and Bakeries

Saint Honore (5 Xuan Dieu, tel. 04/332-355, www.sainthonore.com.vn, 6:30am-10pm daily, VND35,000-200,000) is a charming little Parisian-style bistro, replete with flaky, decadent pastries, fresh bread, and a deli counter that wraps around the end of the building. Delicious sandwiches and crepes feature on the menu alongside a range of coffee and tea options; while there are a handful of more sophisticated meals on offer, it's best to stick to simpler fare, as this is where the café excels. Saint Honore also has a second location (31 Thai Phien, tel. 04/3974-9483, 6:30am-10pm daily) closer to downtown.

SELF-CATERING

Hanoian cuisine is as varied as it is delicious. Those with dietary issues, or those who simply prefer more control in the preparation of their meals, will appreciate shops like Veggy's (99 Xuan Dieu, tel. 04/3719-4630, 8am-8pm daily), a small but well-stocked grocery store near the northern end of West Lake that's packed with familiar Western brands like Kraft, Campbell's, and Betty Crocker. For even more selection, Annam Gourmet (51 Xuan Dieu, tel. 04/3718-4487, www.annam-gourmet.com, 7:30am-8:30pm daily), located in the Syrena Shopping Center, offers a range of useful cooking items and canned goods as well as a small bakery and deli counter, where you'll find several different types of cheese and cold cuts. Prices at both of these shops run on the high side, but you'll find many familiar brand names and a much larger selection than local supermarkets.

If you're simply looking for basic groceries and other essentials, the Hapro Mart (63 Cau Go, 8:30am-10pm daily) in the Old Quarter sells things like pasta, canned goods, and milk. While it's not very big, the store manages to cover most simple ingredients as well as a few toiletries and other odds and ends. There is also a second location (35 Hang Bong, 8:30am-10pm daily) nearby.

Information and Services

TOURIST INFORMATION

You'll find scores of travel agencies boasting "free tourist information" around the Old Quarter, but this local wisdom extends no further than a brochure of the company's tour packages. Your hotel is usually the best place to seek out unbiased travel tips, not to mention other extras like free maps. If you can't seem to track these down, the Tourist Information Center (7 Dinh Tien Hoang, tel. 04/3926-3366, www.ticvietnam.com, 8am-9pm daily) opposite the northern edge of Hoan Kiem Lake provides detailed plans of the city as well as a complimentary Hanoi guide, which lists recommendations on hotels, restaurants, sights, and other attractions in town. While the company operating this office sells its own tours, the free materials on offer make the place a little more helpful than most.

BANKS AND CURRENCY EXCHANGE

You'll find ATMs on nearly every street corner in Hanoi, particularly in the downtown area.

Most hotels and tour agencies offer to exchange currency, as do the majority of banks in the downtown area. Look up the actual exchange rate to ensure that you receive a fair conversion. If you're pressed for time, the bank is your best bet.

Most banks in the capital are open 8am-5pm Monday-Friday. Vietnamese institutions like Vietcombank (www.vietcombank.com.vn) and Sacombank (www.sacombank.com.vn) tend to take a lunch break during the day, shutting their doors 11:30am-1pm; foreign companies like HSBC (www.hsbc.com.vn), Citibank (www.citibank.com.vn), and ANZ (www.anz.com) stay open all day. Some Vietnamese banks are open on Saturday mornings.

While much of the country remains cash-only, you will find that some places in Hanoi, including high-end hotels and upscale restaurants, are beginning to accept credit cards as a form of payment. This is the exception rather than the rule, so check ahead of time. Many businesses tack on a small additional charge for using plastic over paper money.

INTERNET AND POSTAL SERVICES

Hanoi's international post office (6 Dinh Le, tel. 04/3825-4503, www.vnpost.vn, 7am-5pm Mon.-Fri., 8am-5pm Sat.-Sun.) staffs English-speaking employees. For additional services, visit the central post office (75 Dinh Tien Hoang, tel. 04/3825-5948, www.vnpost.vn, 7:30am-6:30pm Mon.-Fri., 8:30am-5:30pm Sat.-Sun.) just next door. You are less likely to find an English speaker, but employees will usually point you in the right direction.

When shipping packages, Hanoi offers three options: the local post, often slow and less reliable, though affordable, or UPS (10 Le Thach, tel. 04/3824-6483, www.ups.com, 8am-noon and 1:30pm-5pm Mon.-Fri., 8am-noon Sat.), and DHL (Le Thach, tel. 01/800-1530, www.dhl.com, 8am-noon and 1pm-6pm Mon.-Fri.). Both shipping companies have offices on the northern side of the central post office, just around the corner from its front door. Unless absolutely necessary, avoid international shipping, as costs quickly add up.

You'd be hard-pressed to find a hotel in town that does not have a desktop computer in the hotel lobby or, at the very least, a Wi-Fi connection. Indeed, most cafés and restaurants offer free wireless Internet for paying customers.

PHONE SERVICE

Many travelers buy a local cell phone for the trip. SIM cards and basic, reliable Nokia phones are widely available, both new and secondhand, from electronics shops around the Old Quarter as well as at The Gioi Di Dong (468-472 Le Duan, tel. 1/800-1060, www.thegioididong.com, 7:30am-10pm daily), with the cheapest options beginning around VND350,000. Once you obtain a phone and SIM card, you'll have to purchase mobile credit, which is found at most local *tap hoa* (convenience stores). The three main cell carriers in Vietnam are Vinaphone, Mobifone, and Viettel, all of whom operate on a pay-as-you-go basis. Credit comes in increments of VND20,000, VND50,000, VND100,000, and VND200,000.

EMERGENCY AND MEDICAL SERVICES

Vietnam employs three separate phone numbers for emergency response services: 113 is meant for police assistance in the event of robberies, traffic accidents, and crime-related incidents; 114 links to the city's firefighters; and 115 covers medical emergencies. None of these hotlines are likely to have an English speaker on the other end and the city's emergency response teams are sluggish at best.

In the event of a medical emergency, the best thing you can do is contact a foreign medical center directly for help. Local facilities like **Hong Ngoc Hospital** (55 Yen Ninh, tel. 04/3927-5568, 8am-5pm daily) are reliable for simple aches and pains. International hospitals such as **Family Medical Practice** (298 Kim Ma, Van Phuc Compound, tel. 04/3843-0748, www.vietnammedicalpractice.com), which staffs experienced English-speaking foreign and Vietnamese doctors, stay open 24 hours and assist with more serious predicaments. **International SOS** (51 Xuan Dieu, tel. 04/3934-0666, www.international-sos.com) provides a similar level of quality, though its pricing can run high.

PHARMACIES

Scores of pharmacies, also known as *nha thuoc tay,* are scattered throughout the Old Quarter and across town. These facilities stock prescription and over-the-counter remedies, as well as products like tampons and contact lens solution. Most downtown pharmacies also employ at least one English-speaking staff member. The **pharmacy** (119 Hang Gai, tel. 04/3828-6782, 8am-9pm daily) located on Hang Gai is a reliable option, as are the several businesses that run along Phu Doan near the cathedral.

DIPLOMATIC SERVICES

While there is a **U.S. Embassy** (7 Lang Ha, tel. 04/3850-5000, www.vietnam.usembassy. gov), all inquiries regarding American citizens must be directed to the Rose Garden Building, where **consular services** (Rose Garden Bldg., 170 Ngoc Khanh, 2nd Fl., tel. 04/3850-5000, www.vietnam.usembassy.gov, 8:30am-11:30am and 1pm-3:30pm Mon.-Thurs., by appt. only) are carried out, around the corner from the embassy. Due to the fact that all visitors must have a scheduled appointment on the books, look at the embassy's website ahead of time in order to discern what you'll need before venturing to this area. Appointments can also be made online. For emergencies, American citizens are advised to contact the embassy and consular services (tel. 04/3850-5000) during business hours; outside of these times, contact the embassy's **emergency hotline** (tel. 09/0340-1991) for assistance.

LAUNDRY

The majority of Hanoi's accommodations provide laundry services at an additional cost, and there is usually a markup for going this route. Standard pricing on the street is around VND25,000 per kilo, while you'll pay upwards of VND35,000 for the convenience of going through your hotel. The turnaround is usually about a day's time; in lousy winter weather be prepared to wait a little longer, as dryers are seldom used and the cold, humid winter months tend to leave everything a little damp.

Getting There

AIR

Flights from around the country and across the globe arrive at Hanoi's **Noi Bai International Airport** (HAN, Phu Minh ward, Soc Son district, tel. 04/3886-5047, www.hanoiairportonline.com), 20 miles north of the city. Several budget airlines, including Jetstar, Air Asia, and Viet Jet, pass through here in addition to a host of other international carriers. Customs and immigration procedures move quickly; those completing pre-approved visa processing should expect to wait in line for a short while before passing through customs inspections. Those traveling domestically from other in-country destinations will be spared this waiting.

Once you've exited the airport, it's about a 45-minute ride into the city by taxi, minibus, or public bus. Many hotels can arrange airport pickup for an additional fee (starting at VND350,000), so long as you contact them in advance.

Taxis from the Airport

The airport is notorious for a host of taxi troubles: drivers quote flat rates that border on extortion or insist that the destination you've presented is closed, full, or for some other reason unavailable in hopes of steering you to another hotel, where they usually receive a kickback. When metered vehicles are available, it is not uncommon for meters to run up the fare at lightning speed. Your best bet is to write down the name and exact address of your hotel before leaving the airport. This way, you have a clear destination to show your driver and, should he or she attempt to take you elsewhere, you are able to politely refuse and point to the place on the paper.

The easiest way to procure a cab from the airport is to walk to the taxi stand (easily visible when leaving the arrivals area), where a flat rate (to downtown) will be posted on the sign out front. Once you have a taxi, confirm again with your driver the exact price as some drivers will still attempt to overcharge. Stick to trusted companies like Mailinh Airport (tel. 04/3822-2666). From the airport to the downtown area should cost no more than VND400,000, but sometimes even the most reputable companies are dishonest.

Airport Minibus

An airport minibus (7am-7pm daily, VND40,000), courtesy of Vietnam Airlines, leaves from Noi Bai when it has enough passengers to make the journey worthwhile, usually every 30 minutes or so. The minibus drops passengers off in front of the Vietnam Airlines office downtown, one block south of Hoan Kiem Lake. While you may have to wait a few minutes at the airport, this is by far the cheapest and most hassle-free option if you are traveling light. Even if your hotel is not within walking distance of the minibus stop, the combined cost of the minibus fare and a cab from downtown Hanoi to your final destination will be less expensive and reduce the risk of being overcharged by a taxi. The same minibuses also travel the reverse route back to the airport, leaving from the Vietnam

Airlines office (corner of Quang Trung and Hai Ba Trung).

Public Bus from the Airport

A public bus (VND5,000) also makes a trip into town from the airport. Bus number 17 travels via the Chuong Duong Bridge and lets off at Long Bien station, in between Hoan Kiem and West Lake, opposite a stretch of the city's ceramic wall. From here, it's less than a mile to the Old Quarter, making the rest of the journey easily walkable, depending upon your luggage; it's just as easy to catch a cab from here. Bus number 7 also departs from Noi Bai, traveling to the western suburbs of the city. For more specific directions to your destination, it's possible to double-check your route with Google Maps, as its representation of the Hanoi public bus system is accurate and far easier than attempting to decipher the route listings on the Hanoi Bus website.

TRAIN

Hanoi's mammoth train station (120 Le Duan, tel. 04/3942-3697, www.gahanoi.com. vn, 8am-5pm daily) serves southern cities like Danang, Nha Trang, and Saigon, in addition to offering an overnight service north to Sapa. Tickets can be purchased through the station directly as well as from the station's website, and they are offered at travel agencies across town. Ask around when booking through a travel agency, as some outfits charge an excessive commission.

Taxis from the Train Station

The train station attracts plenty of cab drivers eager to catch a fare from an unsuspecting or weary traveler, often at several times the actual price. Opt for one of the Mailinh (tel. 04/3833-3333) cabs waiting out front. If you can't find a Mailinh cab, find a driver who will agree upon a fixed price, as rapid-fire taxi meters can turn a few dollars into 10 or 20 before you know it. Expect to pay around VND50,000 for a trip from the train station to Hoan Kiem Lake (10-minute ride). If you can't find someone willing to take a flat rate, walk a block or two away from the station and you'll find that drivers become increasingly more reasonable.

BUS

Hanoi has four separate bus stations scattered around the outskirts of the city. Giap Bat (Giai Phong, tel. 04/3864-1467, 5am-6pm daily) handles all routes heading south to destinations such as Ninh Binh and Hue, while vehicles at Luong Yen (Nguyen Khoai, tel. 04/3972-0477, 6am-11pm daily) and Gia Lam (9 Ngo Gia Kham, tel. 04/3827-1529, 5am-5pm daily) depart for Ha Long and Haiphong on a regular basis. To the west, My Dinh (20 Pham Hung, tel. 04/3768-5549, 4:30am-11pm daily) offers the occasional fare to Lao Cai and other northwestern towns, too.

You can eliminate the hassle of getting out to the station and navigating Vietnamese bus timetables and fare collectors by taking one of the comfy, air-conditioned coach buses that leave from the offices of Sinh Tourist (52 Luong Ngoc Quyen, tel. 04/3926-1568, www.thesinh-tourist.vn, 6:30am-10pm daily) as well as several other local companies, all of which are located in the downtown area. Sinh Tourist has only the Luong Ngoc Quyen location and another on Tran Nhat Duat (64 Tran Nhat Duat, tel. 04/3929-0394, 6:30am-10pm daily). All other signs advertising "Sinh Cafe," "The Sinh Cafe," or "Sinh Cafe Tourist" are impostors. Go to the correct address and look for the blue-and-white logo.

Hoang Long (28 Tran Nhat Duat, tel. 04/3928-2828, www.hoanglongasia.com, 7am-7pm daily) also offers good value tickets. The company has satellite offices at the Luong Yen, Giap Bat, and My Dinh bus stations as well as its Old Quarter office.

Taxis from the Bus Station

If taxis from the airport come with a bad reputation, the cabs loitering outside of bus stations across the city are in an equally poor standing. Before you even step off the bus, there will be a swarm of drivers crowding the vehicle's entrance, just waiting for a tired, confused, or unsuspecting tourist to wander their way. The best thing you can do when stepping off a bus is grab your luggage and beeline for the exit. Ignore the touts, cab drivers, xe om, and anyone else who insists upon giving you a ride and walk to the street. From there, you needn't head more than a block before you find that cab drivers have backed off the hard sell, and it's much easier to pick out a reputable vehicle, insist upon a reasonable metered cab, and set off.

MOTORBIKE

As it rolls into the capital, Vietnam's famous Highway 1 goes by a few different names before splitting in two directions to avoid the city altogether; from here, Ngoc Hoi transitions into Giai Phong and eventually Le Duan, landing you squarely in the heart of town just a few miles from Hoan Kiem Lake. For those arriving from the east, a pair of equally hectic national roads, Highway 14 and Highway 1, come together eight miles outside of the city and head across the Chuong Duong Bridge into town. Travelers from the west will follow Highway 6 directly to the city center, while those coming from the north have a few options. Thang Long Boulevard reaches Hanoi from the northwest, heading in toward Hoan Kiem Lake; there is also an airport road that passes by West Lake before approaching the city from the north. Being an obvious center of activity, no one highway is less crowded than the others. If possible, arrive before or after the evening rush hour.

TAXIS

Taxis in the capital have a less-than-stellar reputation for overcharging tourists, either through hyperactive meters or by making a few extra turns to run up the fare. Companies like Mailinh (tel. 04/3833-3333) and the red-and-blue Taxi Group (tel. 04/3857-5757) are reputable. When hailing a cab downtown, move away from the heavily touristed areas like Ma May or Ly Quoc Su and hop in a taxi near the main road instead, as this will decrease your chances of encountering an opportunist cabbie. Taxis should always be metered; while some drivers attempt to quote a flat rate, these are almost never in your favor and so it's best to stick to the machine. If possible, try to pay with exact change or something close to it, as cab drivers often insist that they don't have small bills in hopes of gleaning a few extra thousand dong from you. Should you find yourself in a situation where you feel as though you're being taken advantage of—the meter is running too high, for example—stop the cab where you are, pay whatever you believe to be fair, and exit the vehicle. Protesting or waiting to negotiate a price may result in more trouble.

XE OM

Walking around the Old Quarter, you will soon become accustomed to the waving hands and calls of "Hello! Motorbike!" that follow travelers around the city. *Xe om* drivers perch on most corners in the downtown area and can be relentless in their sales pitch. Agree upon a fare before hopping on board. From the Old Quarter to most tourist destinations in the area (barring faraway sights like the Museum of Ethnology and West Lake), your fare should not exceed VND40,000. If a particular driver is not willing to budge on the price, find another driver.

The folks that work Hanoi's *xe om* are daredevils, weaving through a hectic web of traffic that hurtles haphazardly down the narrow streets of downtown Hanoi. For safety's sake, insist upon wearing a helmet. Even if most Vietnamese helmets are not up to Western standards, better to have a little protection in the event of an accident than none at all.

CYCLOS

Slow-moving and seemingly less dangerous than their motorized compatriots, cyclos are the vehicle of choice for many travelers, as they give you the opportunity to sit back as you ply the streets of downtown Hanoi without fear of being run over by a motorbike or moving so quickly that your only thoughts are of safely making it to a particular destination. These sluggish, human-powered trikes ferry tourists all over the Old Quarter with occasional jaunts out to the French Quarter or Ba Dinh Square and beyond, depending on the passenger's needs. A standard cyclo trip lasts about an hour, weaving through the narrow downtown streets and allowing you to get a genuine feel of the city without the anxiety of tackling Hanoian traffic on your own. You'll have to bargain for your fare; most hour-long journeys begin around VND100,000. Your driver will be cycling you around with his own two legs, and so you should expect to pay more than you would for a motorized trip.

PUBLIC TRANSPORTATION
Bus

Hanoi's public bus (tel. 04/3747-0403, www.hanoibus.com.vn, 5am-9pm daily, VND5,000-7,000) lines run all over town and are the most cost-effective way to navigate its narrow streets. While maps of the entire system are not readily available, Google Maps accurately plots the city's bus routes, which makes finding the right bus line as easy as plugging your start and end destinations into the website. On the street, all stops are clearly marked with a blue sign bearing the bus number and its route, and fares are posted on the outside of each vehicle. Most rides around the city cost VND5,000. From the northern edge of Hoan Kiem Lake, buses 9 and 14 are especially useful, as these stop either directly in front of or not far from several popular sights, including Ho Chi Minh Mausoleum, the Temple of Literature, the Hanoi Flag Tower, and the Museum of Ethnology. While many of the more common downtown bus routes stop service at 9pm, some stop earlier, around 8pm. Both Google Maps and the Hanoi Bus website have accurate information regarding bus run times.

Electric Car

Dong Xuan Market runs an electric car service (north side of Hoan Kiem Lake, tel. 04/3929-0509, dongxuantours@gmail.com, 8am-10pm daily, VND150,000/car/35 min., VND250,000/car/hour) that ferries passengers around Hoan Kiem Lake and the Old Quarter area. A handful of standard routes are available, stopping at some of the city's more noteworthy landmarks and shopping areas. Electric cars seat a maximum of seven people and, while it is possible to travel with less than seven to a car, you'll have to cover the cost for the entire vehicle regardless of how few or how many individuals are on board.

VEHICLES FOR HIRE

Motorbike rentals are widely available in the downtown area, especially around Ngo Huyen near St. Joseph's Cathedral and along Dinh Liet to the north of Hoan Kiem Lake. Some of the foreign-owned rental outfits attempt to charge as much as VND210,000 per day, but you can just as easily rent a bike of reasonable quality for VND100,000 from one of the Vietnamese shops nearby. There are a handful of outfits on Dinh Liet that rent out vehicles at reasonable prices. Depending upon the business, some shops may request collateral for the vehicle, in the form of either an ID or a cash deposit. Do a lap around the block and check for any issues before setting off for the day and insist upon a helmet for the trip. Though you'll see plenty of locals flaunting this rule, Vietnamese law requires that all drivers wear a helmet when driving and you are eligible to be pulled over if you fail to do so.

Hanoi's traffic is hectic. Much of the Old Quarter lacks streetlights or stop signs. Narrow roads combined with fast-paced driving can easily result in accidents. Only confident, experienced drivers should brave Hanoian traffic. Many streets in downtown Hanoi are one way, and turning right on red is forbidden in the capital city. Not all rules of the road are closely followed by locals, but you should be aware of the rules.

Vicinity of Hanoi

Beyond the city limits, Hanoi's suburbs and surrounding countryside offer a few easygoing day trips. At the heart of the Red River Delta, a pair of booming traditional handicraft villages complement the urban chaos, while a serene pagoda complex southwest of the city affords an altogether different view of northern Vietnam. Jaunts to Tam Coc and Hoa Lu, Ninh Binh's main attractions, are possible, with plenty of tour providers offering day trips to the area.

PERFUME PAGODA

One of over 30 pagodas dotting the mountains of Ha Tay province, the beautifully austere Perfume Pagoda (Chua Huong) (tel. 04/3384-9849, www.lehoichuahuong.vn, 8am-5pm daily, VND50,000 plus boat fare) is Hanoi's most popular day trip destination. Perfume Pagoda, named for the clouds of incense permeating the cave's interior, is located inside a cave at the top of a mountain. Forty miles west of the capital, the pagoda complex sprawls across a series of hills overlooking

Vicinity of Hanoi

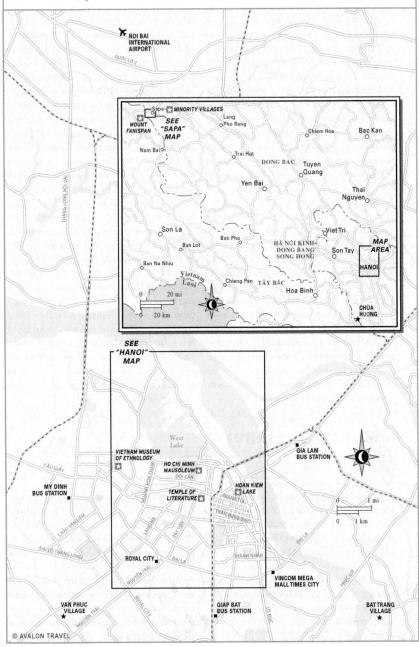

NOI BAI INTERNATIONAL AIRPORT
QUỐC LỘ 2

THĂNG LONG NỘI BÀI

Sapa ★ MINORITY VILLAGES
SEE "SAPA" MAP
MOUNT FANISPAN
Lang
Pho Rang
Chiem Hoa
Bac Kan
Nam Bai
Trai Hut
DONG BAC
Tuyen Quang
Yen Bai
Thai Nguyen
Son La
Ban Pho
Viet Tri
HÀ NỘI KINH DONG BANG SONG HONG
MAP AREA
HANOI
Ban Lot
Son Tay
Ban Na Nhiu
Vietnam Lang
Chieng Pan
TÂY BẮC
Hoa Binh
CHÙA HƯƠNG

0   20 mi
0   20 km

SEE "HANOI" MAP

West Lake

VIETNAM MUSEUM OF ETHNOLOGY
HO CHI MINH MAUSOLEUM
ĐỘI CẤN
GIA LAM BUS STATION
CẦU GIẤY
HOÀNG HOA THÁM
HOAN KIEM LAKE
TRÀNG THI
MY DINH BUS STATION
TEMPLE OF LITERATURE
TRẦN HƯNG ĐẠO
CHÙA VĂN LIÊM
LANG HA
TÂY SƠN
THANH NHAN
ĐẠI LỘ THĂNG LONG
NGUYỄN TRÃI
ROYAL CITY
ĐẠI LA
ĐẠI LA
PHÚC LỢI

0   1 mi
0   1 km

VINCOM MEGA MALL TIMES CITY

VAN PHUC VILLAGE ★
NGUYỄN TRÃI
ROYAL CITY
GIAP BAT BUS STATION
LÒ ĐÚC
BAT TRANG VILLAGE ★

© AVALON TRAVEL

the Yen River and is considered northern Vietnam's most important Buddhist center of worship. Though it's become increasingly more commercial, with the usual roving vendors and boat drivers, the scenery and famous incense-filled grotto are worth a visit for those looking to escape the city.

Most trips to Perfume Pagoda are done via all-inclusive tour. Tour outfitters transport passengers to Yen Vy, a boat station in the town of Huong Son. From here, travelers board a small wooden rowboat (VND40,000/person). The boat glides on a small river past craggy limestone mountains and dense forest, taking about an hour from end to end. When your vessel reaches the pagoda complex, venture through the impressive three-door gate, a stark, towering structure whose black Chinese characters stand out against a bright white background. Past the gates, the temple Chua Thien Tru, also known as Heaven's Kitchen, houses a statue of Quan Am. It's one of the more atmospheric pagodas in the north.

The highlight of the pagoda complex is Huong Tich Cave, which is 164 feet above the water's edge atop a mountain. Though you have the option of reaching Huong Tich on foot, following a winding path up the mountain, most visitors prefer to jump in a bright yellow cable car (VND90,000 one-way, VND140,000 round-trip) to the mouth of the cave, where a set of stone steps descends into the darkened grotto. The cave interior is filled with small altars, obscured by an incense haze, and lacquer effigies. Once you've wandered through, walk back down toward the river. The steps become treacherous in foul weather; you can also hop on the cable car for the return trip. Respectful dress is a must at the complex.

While it's possible to reach the complex on your own via motorbike, the hassle of urban traffic is not really worth the few dollars you might save. Moreover, the journey to Perfume Pagoda is not nearly as picturesque as the sight itself. Dozens of tour companies in Hanoi offer full-day excursions that include

transportation, entry fees, lunch, and a guide for as little as VND530,000.

HANDICRAFT VILLAGES

Across Vietnam, dozens of villages lay claim to culinary specialties or unique traditional crafts. These small, tight-knit communities have produced marble statues, fine silk, traditional Vietnamese lacquerware, or handmade pottery for centuries. Just outside of Hanoi, Bat Trang to the south and Van Phuc to the west each boast a long tradition of producing top-quality items and are known throughout Vietnam for their skilled craftspeople.

Bat Trang

Ten miles south and across the Red River, the small village of Bat Trang has been making high-quality ceramics since the 15th century and is a popular stop for shoppers in search of ceramics. Today, its pottery is nationally famous and exported around the world, with modern-day potters crafting both the traditional blue-and-white ceramics of the past as well as more colorful contemporary designs. Price tags in some of the larger outlets tend not to vary much from those in the city, but you'll find that there is more room for bargaining here and seemingly endless variety.

Most shops (which are also people's houses) are open around 7am-5pm or 6pm daily, and vendors sell similar objects. Visiting Bat Trang is like perusing a large pottery market.

Often, shops will have someone working on pottery, giving a glimpse of the pottery-making process. Ask permission before taking photos, though most shops will likely give permission. If a vendor invites you to try out the pottery wheel or help you make something, there will almost always be an expectation that you buy something in return.

Travelers can reach Bat Trang independently by taxi, bus, or hired vehicle. Bus 47 departs every half-hour from the large bus stop near Long Bien Bridge just north of the Old Quarter off Hang Dau street. Cyclists and motorbikes can reach the area by way of Provincial Road 195 on the eastern bank of the river. When crossing, cyclists should use Long Bien Bridge, while other vehicles should use Chuong Duong Bridge directly south.

Van Phuc

West out of town en route to Perfume Pagoda, the whirring looms of Van Phuc silk village draw droves of curious shoppers exploring the countryside for the day. As early as the 9th century, local residents raised mulberry trees and silkworms here, spinning their fragile cocoons into fabric for sale both in the village and across the country. During the days of the Nguyen dynasty, Van Phuc was required to produce bolts of silk to clothe the royal family. Today, the village houses over a thousand looms and its goods are often exported beyond Vietnam's borders. While shoppers will find the cost of raw material about the same as in the city, ready-made items like scarves, ties, and shirts are notably less expensive here.

Shops generally open at 8am or 9am and close at 5pm daily. Most of the shops in Van Phuc are also workshops. The silk is made there, so you can watch as local proprietors weave different fabrics with a loom. Shop owners are often happy to let you try out the loom, but you will be strongly encouraged to buy something in return.

While most visitors to Van Phuc get here by way of a day tour to Perfume Pagoda, it is also possible to reach Van Phuc independently. Buses 1 and 2 travel out to the village by way of Highway 6, departing from the French Quarter and the lower part of Hoan Kiem district near the train station. Drivers can access Van Phuc via the same route.

Sapa

Perched high above Muong Hoa Valley, the sleepy little town of Sapa is a world apart from its urban contemporaries, quiet and compact amid the vast open space of Vietnam's remote northwest. Now the go-to destination of the region, its rolling hills and verdant, many-tiered rice terraces are the main attraction, coupled with an array of fascinating minority cultures, whose traditional dress, rituals, religious ceremonies, and ways of life continue to exist in much the same fashion as they have for centuries.

Though its tourism industry has seen a boom in recent years, this hilltop town has long captivated visitors, attracting French attention in the early 20th century. Some ethnic Vietnamese moved into the area in the 1960s, but it wasn't until well after the war's end in the 1990s that Sapa saw any major growth spurt.

The fresh air, ample hiking trails, and opportunity for cultural exchange with some of Vietnam's lesser-known communities draw luxury travelers and adventure seekers with the prospect of striking out for minority villages or scaling the colossal Mount Fansipan, Vietnam's tallest peak.

Inclement weather can ruin a visit to Sapa. The best months are September and October, just before the rice harvests take away much of its visual appeal, or at the start of spring, for better views of the valley. From November to February, temperatures plummet, earning Sapa a reputation as the only town in Vietnam that sees snow. In winter, heavy fog makes for poor visibility, spoiling much of the point of a visit to Sapa.

SIGHTS

Sapa town is a peaceful, charming little place, meandering across hillsides and dotted with modest green spaces amid its ever-growing town center. All of its sights are easily accessed on foot, though you'll get a workout traipsing up and down some of the nearby inclines. In the town center, a small park dominated by a monument to Ho Chi Minh leads onto the large local square, a popular gathering place in the mornings and evenings. Farther north near the main highway, Sapa Lake makes for a pleasant stroll, surrounded by manicured gardens and plenty of park benches.

Sapa Market
Nestled in the hillside just below Sapa's main square, the central market (between Fansipan and Cau May streets, 6am-6pm daily) is in full swing from dawn to dusk, alive with vendors hawking bulk items like tea and dried fruit along with fresh produce, meat, and hot meals. A handful of souvenirs and other knickknacks make an appearance, but the stalls set up beneath this market's tented covering stick to the bright and colorful necessities of locals. Even if you're not interested in shopping, it's a pleasant place to wander, as you'll find several items, from greens to tea to certain fruits, which are unique to northwestern Vietnam.

Sapa Museum
Located in a traditional wooden stilt house behind the Tourist Information Center, Sapa Museum (2 Fansipan, tel. 02/0387-1975, 7:30am-11:30am and 1:30pm-5pm daily, free) gives a solid introduction to the town and the area, telling the story of Sapa's history under

the French and its growth as a town during the 20th century. While a handful of the traditions and customs of Sapa's ethnic minorities are touched upon, there's far less background on the H'mong, Dao, Tay, Phu La, and Giay people who inhabit the region. For this, link up with a local guide to learn more about life in the village.

Our Lady of Rosary Church
The diminutive stone Our Lady of Rosary Church (Sapa Town Square, tel. 02/0387-3014, www.sapachurch.org) was first built in 1926 to accommodate Sapa's European parishioners. It is a pretty landmark in town, its gray exterior rounding out the eastern edge of the town square. While the doors are closed outside of mass hours, its steps are often used as a gathering place along with the square nearby.

Cat Cat Village
Cat Cat Village (6am-9pm daily, VND40,000) is home to the Black H'mong. The trip to the village is one of the more accessible walks in the Sapa area. This particular jaunt falls somewhere between a hike and a trek (just over three miles round-trip), with paved, well-trodden paths winding through what is now more of a tourist attraction than

Sapa Lake

Sapa

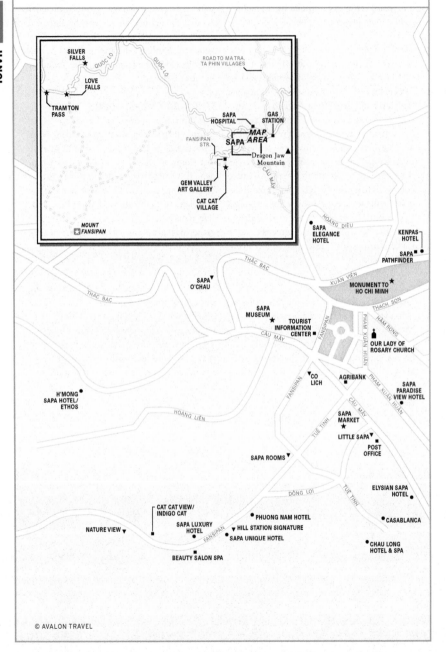

SILVER FALLS
LOVE FALLS
QUỐC LỘ
QUỐC LỘ
ROAD TO MA TRA, TA PHIN VILLAGES
TRAM TON PASS
SAPA HOSPITAL
GAS STATION
FANSIPAN STR.
SAPA
MAP AREA
SAPA
Dragon Jaw Mountain
CẦU MÂY
GEM VALLEY ART GALLERY
CAT CAT VILLAGE
MOUNT FANSIPAN

HOÀNG DIỆU
SAPA ELEGANCE HOTEL
KENPAS HOTEL
SAPA PATHFINDER
THÁC BẠC
SAPA O'CHAU
XUÂN VIÊN
MONUMENT TO HO CHI MINH
THÁC BẠC
THẠCH SƠN
SAPA MUSEUM
TOURIST INFORMATION CENTER
HÀM RỒNG
CẦU MÂY
FANSIPAN
PHAM XUÂN HUÂN
OUR LADY OF ROSARY CHURCH
CO LICH
AGRIBANK
PHAM XUÂN HUÂN
SAPA PARADISE VIEW HOTEL
H'MONG SAPA HOTEL/ ETHOS
FANSIPAN
CẦU MÂY
SAPA MARKET
HOÀNG LIÊN
LITTLE SAPA
POST OFFICE
TUÊ TÌNH
SAPA ROOMS
ĐỒNG LỢI
TUÊ TÌNH
ELYSIAN SAPA HOTEL
CAT CAT VIEW/ INDIGO CAT
PHUONG NAM HOTEL
CASABLANCA
NATURE VIEW
SAPA LUXURY HOTEL
FANSIPAN
HILL STATION SIGNATURE
SAPA UNIQUE HOTEL
CHAU LONG HOTEL & SPA
BEAUTY SALON SPA

© AVALON TRAVEL

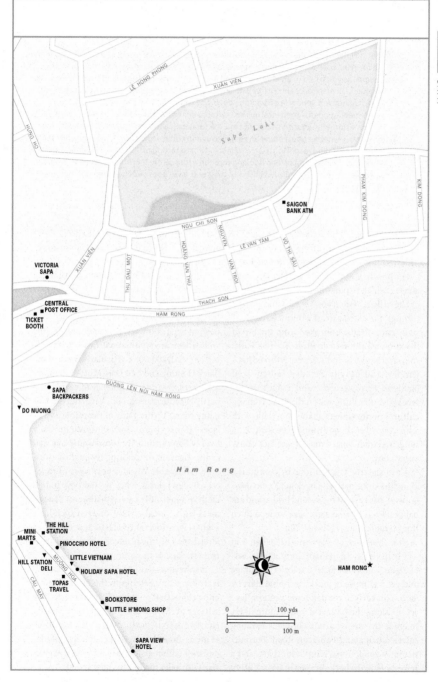

LÊ HỒNG PHONG

XUÂN VIÊN

HÙNG HO

Sapa Lake

PHẠM KIM ĐỒNG

KIM ĐỒNG

■ SAIGON BANK ATM

NGŨ CHI SƠN

HOÀNG VĂN THỤ

NGUYÊN VĂN TRÔI

LÊ VĂN TÁM

VÕ THỊ SÁU

XUÂN VIÊN

THU DẦU MỘT

THẠCH SƠN

● VICTORIA SAPA

CENTRAL
■ POST OFFICE

■ TICKET BOOTH

HÀM RỒNG

ĐƯỜNG LÊN NÚI HÀM RỒNG

● SAPA BACKPACKERS

▼ DO NUONG

Ham Rong

THE HILL
■ STATION

MINI ■
MARTS
■

● PINOCCHIO HOTEL

LITTLE VIETNAM
■ ▼
HILL STATION ▼ HOLIDAY SAPA HOTEL
DELI

MƯỜNG HOA

CẦU MÂY

▼ TOPAS TRAVEL

■ BOOKSTORE
■ LITTLE H'MONG SHOP

HAM RONG ★

SAPA VIEW
HOTEL

0   100 yds

0   100 m

Finding a Guide in Sapa

Budget travelers might find Sapa's tour outfitters out of their price range. The next-best option is to hire an independent local guide in town. While this is decidedly less expensive, it requires extra work, as you'll find many women around Sapa offering to act as guides though few, if any, are certified. On many occasions, a trek with an independent guide turns into a shopping trip, with dozens of handicraft vendors persuading you to part ways with your money.

Recommendations for good local guides can be obtained from your hotel. For extra assurance, spend some time with your guide beforehand. Ask for details about the trip and make your expectations clear—whether you'd prefer an easy hike or a strenuous one, how far you're comfortable walking, whether you're looking to shop or not—prior to setting off.

While it's a greater gamble than booking through a tour outfit, there are independent guides who are great at what they do. Additionally, their entire fee goes directly to them rather than a third party.

an actual village. The walk down to Cat Cat from Sapa affords stunning panoramas of Muong Hoa Valley. En route to Cat Cat's ticket booth, you'll pass by small clapboard houses, which remain the most authentic part of the village. Once you've paid and passed through the entry gate, the line of handicraft stalls runs almost unbroken from the top of the steps all the way down to Tien Sa Falls, showcasing skirts and scarves, T-shirts, hats, jewelry, and heavily detailed indigo-dyed blankets. Across a suspension bridge that teeters above a rushing waterfall, Black H'mong cultural performances (9am-4pm daily with a break for lunch, additional fee), featuring songs and traditional dances, take place nearly every hour.

Complete the Cat Cat loop by continuing along the stone path and back up. *Xe om* drivers wait just beyond the second bridge and are happy to ferry passengers back to Sapa town (for no more than VND40,000).

For shoppers, it pays to visit when Cat Cat is in full swing (10am-2pm), but travelers who simply want to explore the village and get a glimpse of local life should start by 9am. This early in the day, fewer vendors have set up along the path and you're more likely to elude the roving groups of Black H'mong saleswomen along Fansipan Road. For particularly good views, a bit of local art, and a refreshment, the back veranda of Gem Valley

Art Gallery (Cat Cat, tel. 09/1284-9753, 7am-6pm daily, VND25,000-100,000) is a fine spot to rest your legs.

Allow yourself 45-60 minutes to complete the trip there and back.

★ Minority Villages

Beyond Sapa's borders, the surrounding hills and valleys are studded with minority villages (VND20,000), particularly those of the Black H'mong and Red Dao. Most of these remote areas bear a resemblance to each other, partly because many groups have coexisted for many years. Visiting any of the minority villages affords visitors a window into the daily lives of Sapa's minority communities, as well as the pleasure of trekking through the verdant landscape. Wander past rows of modest wooden houses, where women dye indigo cloth or embroider intricate designs. Share a meal with a local family, or even spend the night. Here, several thousand feet above sea level, Sapa's nearby residents are a world apart from the rest of the country.

Just beyond Cat Cat, the next-nearest village, Sin Chai, belongs to the Black H'mong and prides itself on its traditional music. The villages of Ma Tra and Ta Phin to the north, patchwork settlements of Red Dao and Black H'mong households, make equally popular day trips (although locals may be more aggressive with sales pitches in these spots).

Farther south, Ta Van is home to a Giay community not far from Lao Chai village, another Black H'mong settlement, both of which are popular options and can be visited in a single day. Just beyond these two villages is a Red Dao community, Giang Ta Chai, which can also be tacked onto a trek if you're up for the walk. To the east, Hau Thao, Sa Seng, and Hang Da, all Black H'mong villages, are another worthy option for trekkers.

You'll find useful maps of Sapa's vicinity at the local tourism office (2 Fansipan, tel. 02/0387-1975, www.sapa-tourism.com, 8am-5pm daily), which can help you to get the lay of the land.

Hiring a guide (VND200,000-300,000) is a must for these excursions, as you're far more likely to get off the beaten path with a local on hand, and these individuals will have answers for your questions regarding the ins and outs of Sapa's minority cultures. Depending on where you go, a good guide can also help to dissuade villagers from pummeling you with sales pitches. Companies like ETHOS (tel. 09/1679-5330, www.ethosspirit.com) and Sapa O'Chau (8 Thac Bac, tel. 02/0377-1166, www.sapaochau.org, 7:30am-6:30pm daily) run regular tours to several minority villages. On a tour, travelers hike out to the villages and are bused back to Sapa. The walking distance varies based on which villages are visited, ranging 2.5-10 miles. Tours cover no more than three villages in a day, with most going to only one or two (allowing travelers more time in each village).

Many villages can also be accessed by *xe om,* but this takes most of the fun out of the experience, as Sapa's more secluded landscapes are best explored on foot. All villages in the area charge a VND20,000 entry fee for visitors. Homestays and overnight excursions covering several nearby communities can be arranged (with a tour outfitter or freelance guide).

Silver Falls and Love Falls

Just over six miles out of town, a pair of waterfalls line the highway up to Tram Ton Pass. The nearest and most popular is Silver Falls (Thac Bac) (6am-6pm daily, VND10,000), a charming natural sight. It's not worth the walk up to the top, as you can get the gist from the ground. The walk up is a steep set of stairs, but the going is easy.

Farther up the road, Love Falls (Thac Tinh Yeu) (6am-6pm daily, VND30,000) makes more of an impression. Though it's hidden off the highway about a half-mile into the forest, the trek to the falls makes a nice nature walk, strolling through the trees beside Golden Stream (Suoi Vang). You'll need a good pair of shoes and reasonable mobility to reach the end; the stone walkway later deteriorates into a dirt track in some spots, and a few downed trees have crossed the path. The finale, a pretty, moss-covered cascade more than 300 feet tall, makes the journey worthwhile.

Tram Ton Pass

The towering Tram Ton Pass, also known as O Quy Ho, is the highest road in Vietnam, coming in at 1.25 miles above sea level. This never-ending maze of switchbacks teeters on the edge of the Hoang Lien mountains, winding its way from Tam Duong, a small town about 30 miles west of Sapa, up along a narrow, cliff-hugging road before plunging back down to Sapa and, later, Lao Cai. While its highest point, perpetually obscured by dense forest, does not afford the kind of awe-inspiring views you might expect, with time and a motorbike (or, for the very fit, a bicycle) you can venture down the serpentine highway, admiring the view from some of its lower sections. Stop at established pullouts to admire the view and take photos. Drivers on this particular road should exercise great caution, as conditions are risky even in good weather and downright treacherous in foul weather. Take extra care when rounding corners and keep a safe distance from the outside shoulder of the road, as it's a straight drop down.

Dragon Jaw Mountain

Rising above Sapa in the southeast, Dragon

Jaw Mountain (Ham Rong, 7am-7pm daily, VND70,000) affords some pleasant views of town as well as your standard helping of Vietnamese kitsch. The most developed peak in the area, Dragon Jaw bears a spidery network of paths crisscrossing its northern side that look out over the sleepy settlement below as well as toward Fansipan. While it's not exactly a genuine commune with nature, the stone steps that ramble up to the **Cloud Yard,** the platform with the best views of Sapa, are a nice way to pass time on your first day or as you wander around town. Thanks to its paths, solid footwear is not so essential here. You'll want to allow an hour or so to fully explore the winding routes up top. Visitors receive a map of the mountain from the ticket booth; this does little to orient you once you've started on the long stairway up. Regardless, you'll find yourself passing by a restaurant, a rather tired orchid garden, several covered lookouts, a park dotted with statues of the 12 Vietnamese zodiac animals, and, inexplicably, Mickey Mouse.

SIGHTSEEING TOURS

In order to get the most out of exploring Sapa, many travelers sign up for a guided tour to one of the nearby villages, to a bustling local market, or simply deep into the mountains for a homestay. Because so much of Sapa's tourism relies upon connecting with other cultures, it is particularly important to be discerning when choosing a tour company, as you want your experience to be authentic and worthwhile not only on your part but also for the local minorities with whom you interact. There are a handful of trekking and tour outfits in town that focus heavily upon ensuring that the benefits of this region's tourism go directly back to its local residents. If trekking to a nearby minority village is on your itinerary, have a local guide bring you along, as that person will be able to explain the ins and outs of his or her culture better than anyone else.

More than just a trekking outfit, the incredible **Sapa O'Chau** (8 Thac Bac, tel. 02/0377-1166, www.sapaochau.org, 7:30am-6:30pm daily) does as much for the local community as it does for its customers, providing authentic, adventurous treks off the beaten path as well as changing the lives of Sapa's young ethnic minorities. In a region where many minority children do not attend school beyond adolescence, Shu Tan, a young H'mong woman, has made it her mission to afford local students the skills, education, and opportunities that have long eluded this part

view of Sapa from Dragon Jaw Mountain

of the country. Beginning in 2009 as a single homestay in Lao Chai, the Sapa O'Chau outfit operates a school for local students as well as its tour outfit. Training programs assist aspiring tour guides in gaining experience in the field. Sapa O'Chau is a two-way cultural exchange, in which both travelers and community members benefit. The outfit arranges single-day treks (VND252,000-735,000) and multi-day treks (VND840,000-2,625,000) to various villages in the surrounding area, as well as homestays, market visits, and other adventures. The outfit runs a popular café (VND20,000-120,000), which makes some mean fish and chips.

ETHOS (H'mong Sapa Hotel, tel. 09/1679-5330, www.ethosspirit.com, VND525,000-1,680,000) goes to great lengths to ensure that its tours are not only authentic and far-removed for the tourist crowds but that each of its excursions benefits the local community. From treks into the nearby hillside and village visits that don't appear on any other tour company's itinerary, ETHOS focuses on genuine human interactions with activities like sharing a meal or visiting someone's home that lend themselves more to one-on-one interaction. The tour agency operates out of H'mong Sapa Hotel (and thus doesn't have official office hours) and assists with train bookings and longer trips, including a guided tour of the Northwest Loop.

SHOPPING

As the only major tourist town in the northwest, shopping is a popular activity in Sapa, particularly when the fog rolls in to obscure its panoramic views. The main handicraft of the H'mong and Red Dao is textiles; both groups are equally skilled in colorful and detailed embroidery, which often features on skirts, jackets, blankets, bags, and other accessories. Silver jewelry and indigo-dyed items are another specialty of the H'mong. Along Cau May and Muong Hoa streets, plenty of retailers hawk knockoff North Face items for the Fansipan-bound, while handicrafts are virtually everywhere, including on the arms of roving vendors, whose sales pitches range from friendly to downright aggressive.

Hidden beneath the Cat Cat View Hotel, Indigo Cat (46 Fansipan, tel. 09/8240-3647, www.indigocat.dznly.com, 9am-7pm Sun.-Fri.) is a small shop that specializes in Fair Trade products made by H'mong women, namely bracelets, bags, skirts, jewelry, and a few other odds and ends. Look out for the small handouts scattered throughout the store, which explain the significance of many of the intricate patterns you see swirled and looped and stitched across the clothing of local minority women. Indigo Cat also sells pre-packaged DIY sewing kits so that you can make your own H'mong-style bracelet using traditional embroidery patterns. Swing by in the afternoons and one of the shop's owners, a H'mong woman, will help to get you started on the craft with an impromptu sewing class.

The town's only bookstore (Muong Hoa, 8am-7pm daily) hides a short walk down Muong Hoa on the left-hand side. Stocked with photocopied paperbacks and a few genuine books, the shop's titles include old and new English-language favorites. Prices aren't listed, so feel free to haggle, particularly if you purchase more than one item.

SPORTS AND RECREATION

With plenty of green space, rolling hills, and incredible scenery, Sapa is an active destination. Sapa is the home base for trekking day trips to surrounding villages and overnight homestays with local families. These journeys range from leisurely to challenging, with Mount Fansipan being the mother of all treks, but there's also room for cycling and, when the weather takes a turn, a hard-earned massage.

Trekking

With dozens of small communities peppering the mountains and valleys of northwestern Vietnam, gaining access to the more authentic, untouched villages of the area requires at least some travel on foot up the steep inclines of the surrounding hills and along the muddy dirt paths that lead to Sapa's more remote residences. In town, easier walks to Cat Cat Village and around Dragon Jaw Mountain are blessed with paved roads and stone steps. Once you leave town the highway branches off into smaller, rockier trails that bring you away from the buzz of Sapa's tourist center and out to peaceful paddies and stunning mountain vistas. For standard day-long treks and one-night homestays, bring along water and a sturdy pair of shoes. For longer excursions, especially to Fansipan, you'll need to stock up on proper trekking gear. Scores of shops in the area sell North Face goods, most of them knockoffs but some genuine, as well as a host of hiking boots, first-aid essentials, and the like.

Two companies that provide guided treks are Sapa O'Chau (8 Thac Bac, tel. 02/0377-1166, www.sapaochau.org, 7:30am-6:30pm daily) and ETHOS (tel. 09/1679-5330, www.ethosspirit.com).

H'mong children in Cat Cat village

★ MOUNT FANSIPAN

Towering above its surroundings, Mount Fansipan is often referred to as the "Roof of Indochina," standing well above any other peak in neighboring Laos or Cambodia. Looming over the opposite flank of the Muong Hoa Valley, its silhouette can be seen from the town's hillside windows on a clear day and has begun to attract a growing number of ambitious travelers hoping to reach the summit. Though its trails are a little worse for wear, cluttered with rubbish and beginning to get too well-worn for some, the enigmatic mountain remains a point of interest among many adventure-seeking tourists.

Guided excursions to the top can be attempted in as little as a day or as long as 3-5 days, depending upon your level of fitness and your willingness to sleep in the rather damp and dingy camps that hover around 7,000 and 9,000 feet. One-day treks up to the summit are not for the faint of heart: It's a 10-hour hike at best and the gently rolling trails at the start of the journey soon give way to steeper climbs and a final push up to the summit.

Instead, reasonably fit travelers may want to opt for a two-day trip, while those who'd prefer to take their time can venture out into the wild for longer. Shrouded in a bluish haze, the view from 10,311 feet can be fickle even during the summer months, as wind, rain, and other elements have a mind of their own up here. Standing next to the pyramidal marker that signals the end of your uphill climb is well worth the wet shoes and chilly temperatures.

Climbers who sign up for a trip to the top should invest in a sturdy pair of hiking boots and some warm clothes. A decent jacket is still recommended in summer, as the air cools down significantly at this height. Most guided tours begin around VND1,050,000 per person for a single-day excursion, including transportation, entry fees, a guide, and, for overnight trips, a porter or two. When booking your Fansipan trek, it's important to be clear about what's included in the tour, as you'll want to know whether things like water and snacks are provided or you should be packing your own.

Venture into Vietnam's far north and you'll discover another world altogether, awash with rich green rice paddies and wide, flowing rivers that wind around the region's many oversized landscapes. Those who strike out on Vietnam's Northwest Loop will be handsomely rewarded with soaring mountains, plunging valleys, isolated villages, and unfathomable vistas. This is an independent adventure on which you'll find few to no English speakers, no high-end hotels, and not a Western meal to speak of. The views from the northwest's serpentine roads make it well worth the journey.

Starting from Hanoi, this 720-mile circuit runs west toward Dien Bien Phu, the city where Vietnam defeated its French enemies once and for all, turning north past Muong Lay and Lai Chau, before scaling the death-defying cliffs of Tram Ton Pass, rolling into Sapa town, and coasting back down to the capital.

Most travelers make the trip on a motorbike in about a week; cyclists can complete the Northwest Loop in two weeks. Invest in a quality vehicle for the journey, as there aren't many repair shops in the area. What shops do exist have far more experience with motorbikes than multispeed bicycles. Cyclists should stock up on tools, tubes, and other necessities before leaving Hanoi. Before you set off, commit the Vietnamese words for hotel (*khách sạn*, pronounced "cack san"), guesthouse (*nhà nghi*, pronounced "nyah ngee"), and restaurant (*nhà hang*, pronounced "nyah hang") to memory, as these will be essential when you're looking for a place to stop.

Road conditions throughout this region are good, with smooth, sleek asphalt most of the way (with the exception of a treacherous stretch near Muong Lay north of Dien Bien Phu). Opt for heavy-duty tires on both bicycles and motorbikes. Guardrails and barriers are nonexistent. Even though there's little traffic on the roads of the northwest, serious accidents can happen and adequate medical care is a long way away.

A handful of tour outfits in Sapa arrange guided, Easy Rider-style motorbike tours that follow this route, though the cost will be astronomically greater than doing it on your own. You can usually arrange these tours in Hanoi or Sapa and expect to take at least six days to complete the full circuit.

It's highly advised that you pay for the necessary guide for this trek. Going it alone is not only forbidden, but could easily become dangerous, as there is little to direct you once you set out for the summit and, particularly in foul weather, the trail becomes a treacherous, rain-soaked path.

Cycling

There are a small number of local companies that arrange cycling tours or rent mountain bikes to individuals. These excursions are expensive, a fact justified by the quality of the equipment, but then take all the challenge out of the trip by driving travelers uphill before allowing them to roll down to the bottom.

Explore the options from outfitters ahead of time, as some companies offer customized tours.

To combine cycling with a bit of sightseeing, it's possible to rent a mountain bike and blaze your own trail up to Silver Falls and Tram Ton Pass. For more in-depth excursions, book a tour, as the area is remote and finding your way can be difficult without someone to guide you.

Two companies providing bike tours of the area are Sapa Pathfinder (13 Xuan Vien, tel. 02/0387-3468, www.sapapathfinder. com, 6:30am-6:30pm daily) and ETHOS (tel. 09/1679-5330, www.ethosspirit.com). Sapa Pathfinder rents out well-maintained Trek mountain bikes (VND200,000/day).

Massages and Spas

When the fog rolls into Sapa and a heavy mist obscures its picture-perfect views, a popular activity among weary travelers is a trip to the spa. While there are several outfits in town that advertise spa services, including a traditional Red Dao herbal bath, these are hit or miss. For assured quality at a higher price, the spas at both Victoria Sapa (Xuan Vien, tel. 02/0387-1522, www.victoriahotels.asia, 8am-10pm daily, VND630,000-1,260,000) and the Chau Long Hotel (24 Dong Loi, tel. 02/0387-1245, www.chaulonghotel.com, 2pm-10:30pm daily, VND400,000-900,000) provide massage services and other treatments. Non-guests are welcome to visit Victoria's sauna or pool (VND210,000 pp). For a more affordable option, the Beauty Salon Spa (43 Fansipan, tel. 09/7789-3566, 9am-10pm daily, VND120,000-300,000) opposite Sapa Luxury Hotel does a decent job, with quality spa services.

ACCOMMODATIONS

You'll find plenty of excellent mid-range and luxury accommodations lining the two main tourist streets of town, Cau May and Fansipan, not to mention a scattering of other hotels that ramble up the nearby hillside, affording incredible views of Muong Hoa Valley. Thanks to some fierce competition in the area, travelers can look forward to well-appointed rooms, plush furnishings, and a higher level of service in most hotels above the VND525,000 mark. Solo travelers and those on a shoestring are not spoiled for choice. A handful of quality budget hotels offer well-kept rooms at good prices; dorm beds are few and far between, especially if your requirements include clean bedding and bathrooms. A small number of dorm accommodations exist, namely in the budget hotels along Fansipan street.

Under VND210,000

Dorm beds at the Phuong Nam Hotel (33 Fansipan, tel. 02/0350-2633, VND84,000 dorm, VND500,000 double) are some of the most generous in Vietnam, offering a queen-size mattress to weary travelers, along with bright and spacious rooms. En suite bathrooms are small but clean and the back door leads onto a tiny ledge with stunning views of the valley. Hot water and air-conditioning are included in these shared rooms as well as in the hotel's private doubles. If it's privacy you seek, search elsewhere, as the dorm beds represent good value but the private rooms are not up to snuff.

VND210,000-525,000

Amid the jumble of shops and restaurants along Cau May, Elysian Sapa Hotel (38 Cau May, tel. 02/0387-1238, www.elysiansapahotel.com, VND357,000-735,000) represents a solid budget option, with cozy beds, hot water, air-conditioning, TV, Wi-Fi, and tea- and coffee-making facilities in each room. Electric blankets and other accoutrements are available during the winter months. Downstairs, the hotel runs a restaurant as well as a travel desk and assists with tour arrangements.

Looking out over the local park, Kenpas Hotel (11 Xuan Vien, tel. 02/0387-2692, www.kenpas.com, VND252,000-315,000, breakfast included) offers exceptionally good value for money, with large, well-kept guest rooms that come either with or without a window, the former affording decent views of town. Modern amenities like TV, Wi-Fi access, hot water, fans, and heaters are included in each room, as is plush bedding and a clean, spacious bathroom. Downstairs, the hotel runs a tour outfit as well as a shop specializing in high-quality trekking gear. The staff are a friendly, easygoing crowd.

The friendly folks at Casablanca (26 Dong Loi, tel. 09/7441-8111, www.casablancasapahotel.com, VND336,000-630,000) offer decent guest rooms with standard amenities such as air-conditioning, hot water, TV, Wi-Fi, and tea- and coffee-making facilities. The staff is especially cheerful and service-minded, and the location, wedged between the larger tourist streets of Cau May and Fansipan, provides a break from the shops and activity nearby. Breakfast is included in the room rate, but it is possible to book accommodations without the additional cost.

VND525,000-1,050,000

Amid the droves of accommodations

Sapa Luxury Hotel

(46 Fansipan, tel. 02/0387-1946, www.cat-cathotel.com, VND630,000-1,260,000, breakfast included) is in its name. Rising above the smaller buildings across the street, this hotel boasts some incredible views of the valley and, while its rooms are basic, you'll find hot water, air-conditioning, TV, and Wi-Fi among the hotel's amenities, along with electric blankets for the winter months and additional services, such as DVD players and space heaters, available for rent. Discounts are sometimes available for multi-night stays.

While the **Sapa Unique Hotel** (39 Fansipan, tel. 02/0387-2008, www.sapauniquehotel.com, VND735,000-1,155,000) is as good as any on the block, its staff set the place apart with top-notch service and a genuine effort to ensure that travelers enjoy their stay. Rooms are cozy and well-appointed, featuring hot water, air-conditioning, Wi-Fi, television, and modern furnishings. The attached travel outfit, Viet Sapa, is notably reliable.

Tucked off the town's main square, **Sapa Elegance Hotel** (3 Hoang Dieu, tel. 02/0388-8668, www.sapaelegancehotel.com, VND735,000-840,000, breakfast included) earns top marks for its location, overlooking the valley but just far enough removed to lie beyond the reach of Sapa's touristy streets. Outfitted in cozy, modern furnishings, each guest room features hot water, Wi-Fi access, television, a dual air-conditioning and heating system, minibar, in-room safe, and tea- and coffee-making facilities. The hotel's pleasant staff assist with tours and travel arrangements.

VND1,050,000-2,100,000

A breathtaking view of the valley and mountains rolling off into the distance win **H'mong Sapa Hotel** (10 Thac Bac, tel. 02/0377-2228, www.hmongsapahotel.com, VND1,050,000-2,310,000, breakfast included) huge points, complemented nicely by the friendly service, restaurant, mountain view terrace, and excellent tour outfit. Superior accommodations are well-furnished with hot water, TV, Wi-Fi, and an air-conditioning system that blows hot

overlooking the valley, ★ **Sapa Luxury Hotel** (36 Fansipan, tel. 02/0387-2771, www.sapaluxuryhotel.com, VND588,000-1,890,000, breakfast included) stands out for its exceptional hospitality. This family-owned boutique hotel is just a stone's throw from several of the town's main attractions, including Cat Cat Village, the local market, and Cau May shopping street. All rooms are clean and spacious, featuring walk-in showers and twin- or queen-size beds. Rooms are equipped with a mini-bar, television, computer, and Wi-Fi. A complimentary Vietnamese or Western breakfast is served each morning. Depending on the season, it's best to book early, as there are only 10 rooms. The hotel offers pickup service from the train station in Lao Cai for those who call ahead. For budget travelers, small but tidy rooms are available in the back without a mountain view, but for the full experience book a room in the front, where the balcony offers breathtaking panoramas of the valley and Mount Fansipan.

The reason for the success of **Cat Cat View**

Learn to Cook the Sapa Way

The Hill Station Signature restaurant (37 Fansipan, tel. 02/0388-7111, www.thehillstation.com) runs a **H'mong cooking class** (VND580,000) for culinary-minded travelers. During the class, you'll visit a local market to pick out ingredients, work with an English-speaking chef, and learn how to create a menu of five H'mong dishes. Students also visit a farm in nearby Hau Thao village, run by a local family, where the restaurant gets all of its ingredients.

and cold. For a private balcony, upgrade to a deluxe room. Booking directly with the hotel tends to get you a discount.

Perched on the hillside above Cau May, the Sapa Paradise View (18 Pham Xuan Huan, tel. 02/0387-2684, www.sapaparadiseviewhotel.com, VND900,000-1,720,000, breakfast included) wins top points for service. Rooms are comfortable and well-appointed, with an in-room safe, television, Wi-Fi access, hot water, and an in-room computer. The upper floors afford pleasant views, while certain rooms also include a private balcony. The hotel assists with booking tours and other travel arrangements. Its ground-floor restaurant is a popular choice, with delicious barbecue and hotpot gracing the menu.

Over VND2,100,000

A beautiful, well-hidden resort overlooking this sleepy town, Victoria Sapa (Xuan Vien, tel. 02/0387-1522, www.victoriahotels.asia, VND4,000,000-6,000,000) boasts 77 rooms, a private terrace, and stunning views of the surrounding area thanks to its hillside perch. Spacious accommodations include TV, Wi-Fi access, air-conditioning, hot water, and tea- and coffee-making facilities. Superior, deluxe, and suite rooms are available, some of which come with private balconies. The resort counts a top-notch restaurant, bar, spa, fitness center, kids club, tennis court, and indoor heated pool in its offerings.

FOOD

You won't find too many regional dishes in this foggy northern town, but local favorites include miniature barbecue skewers, which

make for an excellent afternoon snack, as well as roast suckling pig, which you'll find on a spit in front of a few eateries in town. Though it's not native to the area, trout has become a popular local commodity. Sapa's minority groups also have some dishes of their own. Most restaurants in town seem to hold to the notion that Western travelers would prefer Western food, and so it can be tricky to find more authentic Vietnamese fare, though one or two restaurants in Sapa town excel at providing genuine homegrown meals. For cheaper options, stick to the market stalls, as Sapa's eateries, almost all of which cater to foreign tourists, come at a price.

Clustered around the foot of Dragon Jaw Mountain beneath a maze of tarpaulins are several *do nuong* (barbecue) vendors (mid-morning-late afternoon daily, VND5,000-10,000/skewer). These tiny stalls are no more than a single miniature grill and a few tables. The colorful displays of skewers, packed with everything from pork and veggies to chicken wings, dumplings, and tofu, are enticing after a long walk up the mountain. Often accompanied by bamboo tubes of sticky rice, these tasty morsels are enjoyed as a snack or alongside a few drinks and hit the spot during cold, rainy weather.

A local restaurant, Co Lich (1 Fansipan, tel. 09/1282-8260, 7:30am-midnight daily, VND60,000-300,000), at the top of Fansipan street, does a tasty suckling pig, which appears on the rotating spit out front. Beyond pork, you'll find a slew of Vietnamese meat and vegetable dishes on its extensive menu, all at reasonable prices.

Though it's nearly invisible from outside,

tucked soundly beneath the Sapa Paradise View Hotel is its restaurant, Paradise View Restaurant (Sapa Paradise View Hotel, 18 Pham Xuan Huan, tel. 02/0387-2683, www.sapaparadiseviewhotel.com, 6:30am-9pm daily, VND250,000-365,000), a cozy little spot that prides itself on serving only top-notch barbecue and hotpot dishes. Diners in the mood for authentic local fare will appreciate the restaurant's select offerings, namely the mouthwatering salmon hotpot, whose ingredients are picked fresh from a tank at the back of the restaurant, not to mention the cheerful and conscientious staff.

The charming Little Sapa (18 Cau May, tel. 02/0387-1222, 8am-9pm daily, VND45,000-135,000) may well be one of the most affordable eateries in a town of tourist-heavy restaurants. Its well-rounded menu of Vietnamese dishes showcase a more genuine version of Vietnamese cuisine and, while Little Sapa's clientele is largely foreign, the prices and tastes are more local than its competition. Indoors, embroidered tablecloths and plenty of festive lighting add some cheer, and the staff are an industrious and friendly bunch.

Little Vietnam (33 Muong Hoa, 8:30am-last customer daily, VND45,000-190,000) operates out of a tiny, cozy wooden storefront along Muong Hoa just opposite the Bamboo Sapa Hotel. Vietnamese cuisine takes up most of the menu, offering more than just your standard backpacker fare, with a few burgers and sandwiches rounding out the list. Staff are friendly, and most prices manage to come in under VND100,000, making this one of the more affordable spots in the tourist area.

Perched on the hillside overlooking Muong Hoa Valley, Nature View (51 Fansipan, tel. 02/0387-1438, 8am-10pm daily, VND60,000-125,000) boasts some of the best views in town, not to mention an extensive list of Vietnamese fare, including chicken, beef, pork, fish, duck, deer, and wild boar. An especially tasty vegetarian set menu is also on offer for lunch and dinner. Regardless of whether you come for a full-blown meal or just an afternoon drink, the breathtaking panoramas from Nature View's dining room are what set the place apart, with large windows and an open-air rooftop affording a clear sight to the valley below.

The chic and omnipresent Hill Station (7 Muong Hoa, tel. 02/0388-7111, www.thehillstation.com, 8am-10pm daily, VND75,000-275,000) is clearly doing well for itself, as the trendy eatery now counts a deli, boutique, and signature Vietnamese restaurant in its offerings around town. At its main venue, an exposed brick building just near the foot of Cau May, you'll find deli-style sandwiches, pastries, cheese, and charcuterie on the menu, while the small black-and-white boutique down the road stocks jars of Sapa honey, tea, genuine H'mong jewelry, and other souvenirs.

For an upscale and authentic meal, the ★ Hill Station Signature (37 Fansipan, tel. 02/0388-7111, www.thehillstation.com, 8am-10pm daily, VND70,000-145,000) showcases a host of dishes unique to Sapa's minority cultures, from banana flower salad to fried chicken with wild ginger and smoked pork belly. Vegetarian options are available, taking advantage of several mountain greens you won't find elsewhere in Vietnam, along with homemade tofu. Throw in a bit of rustic chic, with low tables and mounds of hemp as seat cushions, simple porcelain, and a killer view of the valley, and Hill Station Signature is easily one of the best eateries in town. Higher tables are also available.

Chefs at the cozy, corner-side Sapa Rooms (18 Fansipan, tel. 02/0650-5228, www.tet-lifestyle-collection.com, 6am-7pm daily, VND40,000-80,000) excel in the art of breakfast, serving up thick, golden-brown slices of French toast, sweet corn fritters, lemon souffle pancakes, and wholesome homemade muffins not only in the morning but throughout the day. You'll find top-notch European coffee here, as well as an array of oddly shaped furniture, H'mong-patterned decorations, and other contemporary art. Prices are reasonable, though portions run on the small side.

INFORMATION AND SERVICES

Sapa's Tourist Information Center (2 Fansipan, tel. 02/0387-1975, www.sapa-tourism.com, 8am-5pm daily) is one of the more helpful of its kind, dispensing free advice and maps with a smile. Tours can be arranged without the hard sell you might find elsewhere.

The only bank located in the more touristy part of town is an Agribank (Cau May, tel. 02/0387-1107, www.agribank.com.vn, 7:30am-11:30am and 1:30pm-5pm Mon.-Fri.) on Cau May, which also has an ATM next door. Should you run into any trouble with this machine, you can find a Saigon Bank ATM (corner of Ngu Chi Son and Vo Thi Sau) farther into town, near the lake outside the Riverside II Hotel.

Sapa's post office (20 Cau May, tel. 02/0387-1247, 8am-5pm and 6pm-8pm daily) runs a small branch near the market that can handle mail and postal services for travelers. For more in-depth queries, swing by the central post office (6 Thach Son, tel. 02/0387-1298, 7am-9pm daily).

The local hospital (Dien Bien Phu, tel. 02/0387-1237) sits on the northern edge of town. But, medical care in the remote northern mountains is well below par compared to Vietnamese cities. In the event of an emergency and for any serious issues, head back to Hanoi.

GETTING THERE

By Bus

Buses to Sapa can be tricky to find. Hung Thanh (162B Tran Quang Khai, tel. 04/3633-7575, www.hungthanhtravel.vn, 8am-7pm daily, VND300,000) is a reliable company that runs overnight sleeper buses from Hanoi to Sapa and vice versa. Buses leave in the early evening and arrive in the wee hours of the morning right beside Sapa Lake. For the return trip to Hanoi, book your seat through the ticket booth (6 Thach Son, tel. 09/1486-4126, 7am-9pm daily) outside Sapa's central post office. There's just one ticket vendor, who may be out when you're there. Phone for someone to sell you the ticket if that happens.

While a handful of bus companies operate buses back to Hanoi, you'll want to be discerning in which one you choose, as the mountain road leading to Sapa is winding and narrow; safe, experienced drivers are an absolute must. Hung Thanh is your best bet above the others.

By Train

When heading to Sapa, the preferred method

Hill Station Signature

of travel is by sleeper train. Bare-bones hard sleeper cabins feature a single thin palette accompanied by a worn blanket and pillow. For more comfort, a number of private companies run plush, soft sleepers equipped with air-conditioning, comfier mattresses, and cleaner bedding. A lower berth ticket allows you to be closer to your belongings, which will inevitably be slid underneath the bottom bunk; while it's not especially common, theft does occur on sleeper trains.

Ticket prices among Hanoian travel agents vary drastically based on the agent's fee; ask around before settling on an agency. For the best possible fare, buy your ticket from the train station. Lines and organization are not a major focus at the ticketing counter, but there are one or two agents who speak English and can help to arrange your trip. The journey from Sapa to Hanoi is easier to sort out, with the **ticket booth** (6 Thach Son, tel. 09/1486-4126, 7am-9pm daily) outside the central post office quoting some of the better rates in town. The route back to Hanoi is mysteriously more expensive: where you can find a hard sleeper from Hanoi to Sapa at about VND450,000, you'll be paying at least VND600,000 for the same trip in the opposite direction. The commission attached to train tickets in Sapa runs VND40,000-100,000.

The final stop for northbound trains is not Sapa (which does not have a train station), but the **Lao Cai train station,** roughly 23 miles northeast of town near the Chinese border. From Lao Cai, get to Sapa by taking a minibus. The standard fare for a trip from Lao Cai to Sapa city center is VND50,000.

There are enough minibuses around that you can walk away from anyone who attempts to overcharge. Before paying, get confirmation that the tout leading you to a particular minibus is affiliated with that vehicle—with so many people around, it's easy to pay your fare up-front, only to find that the tout involved is in no way affiliated with that minibus. Wait until you reach town before handing over the fare.

GETTING AROUND
Taxis and *Xe Om*
Plenty of *xe om* drivers hang out near the town square, waiting to offer a ride or rent a motorbike to you. For larger vehicles, call a **Fansipan** (tel. 02/0362-6262) taxi. Keep in mind, most everything in Sapa is within walking distance and there are few scenarios in which you'd need to take a cab, with the exception of Silver Falls.

Vehicles for Hire
Walking around downtown Sapa, you'll see tons of hotels and independent enterprises renting motorbikes to travelers. Semi-automatic vehicles run around VND80,000 per day, while an automatic will set you back VND100,000 a day. Check the brakes and all other functions of the bike before taking off, as roads are steep and medical attention is far away. While traffic may move slower on the uphills, many a truck or motorbike will come racing down an incline at top speed, not always on the appropriate side of the road, and locals often walk along the shoulder of the highway.

Ha Long Bay and the Northern Coast

Boasting wild, uncharted jungles and karst-studded seas, Vietnam's northern coast captivates travelers with its breathtaking scenery. Whether on water or land, the otherworldly landscapes of the region provide a stunning backdrop for adventure.

Ha Long Bay (literally, Bay of the Descending Dragon) is the country's most famous attraction, entrancing millions of visitors each year to tour its islands and caves. The placid waters of the bay are awash with luxury cruise liners and modest wooden junk boats that spill over into Ha Long's smaller and less crowded neighbors, Lan Ha Bay and Bai Tu Long Bay. Jagged, rocky islands pepper the seascape, along with hundreds of weatherworn grottoes, making this one of the most photogenic places in Vietnam.

Blanketed in dense green jungle and razor-sharp limestone peaks, the majority of Cat Ba, Ha Long's largest island, remains untouched, rounding out the western edge of the bay. Here you can lounge on a quiet beach or trek through the jungle in a national park, looking out for the island's varied wildlife.

Where Ha Long is often overrun with tourist junk boats and foreign travelers, the smaller, quieter Lan Ha Bay, located off Cat Ba Island's eastern shores, remains wonderfully unencumbered. The area's trademark limestone karsts rise dramatically out of the sea in sharp, striking ridges and rippled rock faces, their bases worn away by erosion. Lush jungle foliage sprouts from the porous rocks, seemingly growing out of nothing, and if you're lucky you may catch a monkey or two swinging between the trees.

Farther south near Ninh Binh are the mesmerizing karsts of Tam Coc and Trang An, affectionately nicknamed "Ha Long Bay on Land." This region is growing more popular with tourists, and functions as a great base from which to explore northern Vietnam.

HISTORY

For thousands of years, the waters of the north coast played a crucial role in ancient Vietnamese history, with several significant military victories taking place on the Bach Dang River just west of Ha Long Bay. In

---

Previous: Cuc Phuong National Park; Ha Long Bay. **Above:** rocky island in Lan Ha Bay.

Look for ★ to find recommended
sights, activities, dining, and lodging.

Highlights

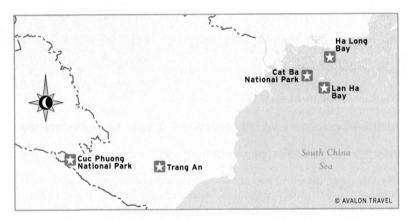

© AVALON TRAVEL

★ **Ha Long Bay:** Relax amid the placid waters and craggy, mist-drenched islands of Vietnam's most storied natural wonder (page 81).

★ **Cat Ba National Park:** Kayak, climb, and hike through the tangle of dense green jungle, still wild and untouched, that extends across the island's northern half and into the bay beyond (page 88).

★ **Lan Ha Bay:** Take in stunning, mist-covered views among the limestone giants of this bay, a captivating miniature version of Ha Long (page 92).

★ **Trang An:** Explore limestone karsts, water-logged paddy fields, ancient temples, and tunnel-like caves in what's called "Ha Long Bay on Land" (page 113).

★ **Cuc Phuong National Park:** With a handful of independent hikes and a top-notch primate conservation center, this park brings adventure and an up-close look at endangered Cat Ba and Delacour's langurs (page 119).

Ha Long Bay and the Northern Coast

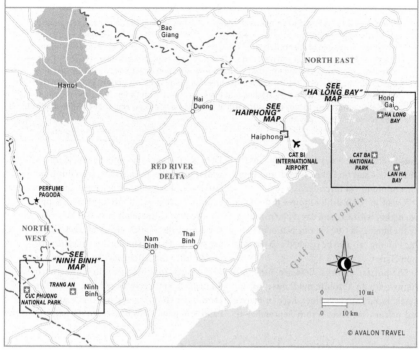

AD 938, emperor Ngo Quyen famously defeated the Chinese in this very place by planting sharpened ironwood spikes beneath the water, which rendered his enemy's vessels immobile when the tide went out. This victory allowed Ngo Quyen to begin the first major Vietnamese dynasty.

By the 12th century, Ha Long Bay was a successful international trading port, drawing in merchants from near and far, though it was still occasionally used for military purposes. Vietnamese revolutionaries used the caves nestled deep within the bay's limestone karsts during the Franco-Vietnam and American Wars. Hospitals and meeting halls were set up inside the dank confines of these underground chambers, many of which remained undetected by enemy forces.

Today, the bay has traded its duties as a military and commercial port for a starring role in the region's tourism, with dozens of white junk boats gliding across the water. Few of Vietnam's attractions have achieved the level of international recognition bestowed upon Ha Long Bay, where even the off season teems with domestic and foreign travelers.

PLANNING YOUR TIME

A visit to Ha Long Bay can take as little as two days or as long as four, depending upon your enthusiasm for on-the-water adventure. Most travelers—particularly those on a shorter schedule—opt for Ha Long Bay or Ninh Binh, as Ninh Binh also goes by the nickname "Ha Long Bay on Land."

In Ha Long Bay, how you travel plays a role in the amount of time you'll need. For a day cruise on the bay, devote two days of travel to arrive in Ha Long city, book a cruise, go on the cruise, and return to Hanoi. For an overnight

The Legend of Ha Long Bay

The name Ha Long Bay, also known as the "Bay of the Descending Dragon," has been around for centuries. The story goes that, in the early days of Vietnam, attacks by sea were a constant threat for the people of the north coast. Seeing their plight, the Jade Emperor, a god-like figure, dispatched Mother Dragon and her children to protect the Vietnamese people. As enemy ships sailed into the bay, preparing for attack, the dragons swooped down, spitting jade pearls into the water, which instantly turned to stone. The treacherous maze of limestone islands caught the enemy ships off guard and they crashed into the rocks. Once the invaders had been defeated, Mother Dragon chose to stay on earth, settling down in Ha Long Bay, while her children made their home nearby in Bai Tu Long.

cruise, set aside 2-3 days, depending on the cruise. For a stay on Cat Ba Island, give yourself a minimum of three days.

A visit to Ninh Binh requires just one or two nights, with an extra day if you're keen to see the langurs at Cuc Phuong National Park. Cuc Phuong can also be reached as a day trip from Hanoi.

The hottest months, between June and August, are an absolute madhouse, as domestic holidaymakers flock here in droves and prices skyrocket. From September to December, things quiet down considerably, while the weather holds steady. Traveling from late December to late February promises a slightly more peaceful atmosphere, though hundreds of Chinese tourists still skip over the border for a quick visit and weekenders arrive from Hanoi. During this time, inclement weather can often sideline boat cruises in Ha Long. Your best bet is to visit between September and early December, when the crowds are thinning out and the weather is calm enough to allow boats onto the bay.

Ha Long Bay and Vicinity

An enigmatic maze of blue-green waters and jagged limestone karsts, Ha Long Bay is the most well-known attraction in the country. Millions of years in the making, this aquatic enclave off the northern coast boasts a staggering 1,969 islands, countless caves, and over 2,000 different species of plant and animal life. Particularly in the colder months, when a dreary mist hangs heavy over the craggy islands and creaking wooden boats of the bay, it's hard not to be drawn in by the mystery of Ha Long.

Beyond its worldwide reputation for captivating scenery—it was voted one of the New 7 Wonders of Nature in 2011—the bay holds great historical significance. Scholars believe Ha Long housed no less than three prehistoric cultures, stretching its history several thousand years into the past. During the 10th and 13th centuries, monumental battles were fought here, including revered general Tran Hung Dao's defeat of Mongol forces in 1288 and the demise of the Han Chinese under Ngo Quyen in 938.

While much of Ha Long's beauty remains, tourism has impacted the area. Many tourist boats are packed onto the same handful of sightseeing routes, and there's more than a little trash floating in the placid water. Local residents have borne the brunt of the bay's popularity as well. Ha Long maintains a few small fishing communities, whose floating houses populate the quieter corners of the bay. These families will soon be forced to move as the government attempts to clear the area for increased tourism.

Ha Long Bay and Vicinity

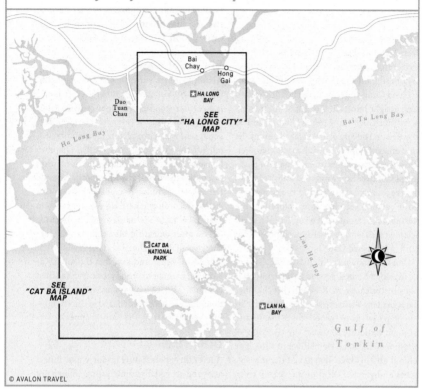

© AVALON TRAVEL

★ HA LONG BAY

Ha Long Bay is home to caves, islands, a few small beaches, and sleepy fishing villages. Between the leisurely pace of the bay's cruise boats (a result of the high volume of traffic) and the sheer number of islands in the area, it's impossible to reach all of Ha Long's attractions on a single trip. Most overnight cruises do a nice job of hitting the more noteworthy spots. Because the bay is accessible only by boat tour, you'll have little to no control of which sights you see once you've booked your trip. Check cruise company itineraries for particular attractions before booking. The entry fee for each cave (VND50,000) is usually included in the price of the cruise.

Thien Cung Cave

Thien Cung Cave (8am-5pm daily), or Heaven Palace, sees droves of tourists each day shuffling along its 623-foot path, which winds around towering, distorted stalagmites and beneath spiky, ridged formations that dangle from above. Now one of the most popular attractions in the bay, not to mention the closest to shore, Thien Cung has lost a bit of its natural luster as a network of neon fluorescent lights and the constant flashbulbs of cameras illuminate the interior, but it's still an impressive sight. Its 32,292-square-foot interior consists of two floors, both of which were formed 7,000- 11,000 years ago. (Visitors are only permitted to wander the top level.) The sheer number of people packed into Thien Cung can feel like cattle being herded through the line.

Dau Go Cave

Dau Go Cave (8am-5pm daily) remains obscure, often overlooked on boat tours. Where visitors step off the narrow path leading out of Thien Cung and back to the boating docks, hang a right into Dau Go, about 100 meters away from Thien Cung; you will find it far less crowded and devoid of artificial additions. Its wide entrance opens onto the first chamber, a bright and cavernous room. A narrow pathway passes over limestone and under slender, bizarre stalactites, traveling the perimeter of the cave's three chambers before looping back out to the front, where you'll find a small stele engraved with the words of emperor Khai Dinh, who visited Dau Go in 1918.

Dau Go, known in English as the Cave of the Wooden Stakes, gets its name from a famous historical event. It was in this chamber that legendary Vietnamese general Tran Hung Dao prepared the ironwood stakes that he and his men would use to defeat the last Mongol invasion on the Bach Dang River in 1288. The general and his men sharpened the massive spikes and planted them in the nearby river,

just deep enough to be invisible during high tide. When the Mongol ships sailed down the Bach Dang and the tide ebbed, they became trapped, propped up on a bed of spikes, and easily defeated by Vietnamese forces.

Sung Sot Cave

Also known as Surprise Cave or Amazing Cave, Sung Sot Cave (8:30am-4:45pm daily) is a regular stop on overnight cruises. From its large opening, several steps and 82 feet above sea level, to the picturesque landing just outside the exit, Sung Sot's vaulted chamber houses a variety of formations. One formation resembles the Buddha, while another, beside the cavern's entrance, resembles a horse with a sword. According to local legend, this is where Thanh Giong, a Vietnamese folk hero, came to rest after defeating his enemies. The legend goes that when he died, Thanh Giong left behind his horse and sword at the mouth of Sung Sot in order to protect the cavern against demons. This cave's expanse is impressive, though it can get crowded, and artificial lighting takes away from the natural appeal.

Other Caves

A few other spots feature on some tour itineraries and are equally as interesting, though not

Ha Long Bay

Choosing a Ha Long Bay Tour

Not every cruise ship or tourist boat plying Ha Long Bay is worth the cost. Here are some tips for booking your overnight stay in the bay.

Expect to spend more money for a quality tour. The extra money spent on a cruise with a reputable company can make a monumental difference in the safety, quality, and value of your experience. Any cruise company that offers a rate at or below VND2,100,000 is probably using an aged fleet.

The brochures are too good to be true. Every booking office and travel agency in Hanoi (where most Ha Long trips are arranged) will show you glossy photos of beautiful wooden junk boats and plush beds sprinkled with rose petals. While mid-range and luxury cruise boats tend to match their promotional materials, don't be fooled: More than a few of the budget cruise brochures are either outdated or false. A clue: All boats in Ha Long Bay are painted white.

Choose safety first. A handful of sinkings have occurred in the last decade, most recently in 2011, when 11 foreign tourists and a Vietnamese guide drowned due to poor boat maintenance. Though accidents and fatalities are rare, cheaper cruises tend to use poorly maintained boats, so there is a risk inherent in choosing a lower-priced option.

Know the cancellation policies. Make sure the tour provider clearly outlines its policies regarding weather-related cancellations. Authorities will sometimes shut down the bay (particularly November-January), ordering all boats off the water due to inclement weather. Ask exactly which costs are reimbursed and how the situation will be handled to avoid any further complications.

---

as popular as the most-visited caves. One of these is **Golden Tortoise Cave (Dong Kim Quy)**, teeming with stalactites. According to local legends, this cave is the final resting place of Hoan Kiem Lake's tortoise, a petrified stone formation deep inside the cave.

In the early 15th century, Vietnamese emperor Le Thai To used a magical sword to defeat Chinese invaders. Following his victory, the emperor was rowing on Hanoi's Hoan Kiem Lake when a giant tortoise swam up to his boat, took the sword in its mouth, and disappeared beneath the surface. (This event earned Hoan Kiem Lake its name, which translates to Lake of the Returned Sword.) The tortoise took the blade back to Ha Long Bay where it encountered evil spirits and was forced to defend itself. Though it defeated the assailants, the tortoise was so exhausted that it found a cave in which to rest and soon after turned to stone. Today, visitors rub its back for good luck.

Follow the path through the stalactite and stalagmite formations, and you'll pass the tortoise toward the end of the path.

Another storied set of caves are **Virgin Cave (Dong Trinh Nu)** and the adjacent **Drum Cave (Dong Trong)**, named after a pair of unrequited lovers. The tale goes that there was a beautiful woman who loved a young fisherman. The couple hoped to marry, and so one day the young man set off to sea in order to catch fish for their wedding day. While the young man was away, the girl's family, who was very poor, sent their daughter to live with a rich man. Devastated, the young woman refused to go, and her wealthy suitor exiled her to a small island in the bay, where she turned to stone. When the young man heard that she was in danger, he began searching for his lover. From his boat, he shouted as loud as possible but could not make himself heard over the weather, which had turned into a terrible storm. Wet and exhausted, he too turned to stone. In Virgin Cave, the formation is of a young woman lying down with her hair falling over her head, looking toward the sea. In Drum Cave, the formation is of a young man with his face turned toward Virgin Cave, as if calling to the woman. Cruise boats (including Gray Line boats) often stop outside the caves, as guides relate the story of the lovers. Tours don't usually let passengers disembark to explore these caves.

The small Me Cung Cave occasionally makes it onto tour itineraries. Its contents offer fascinating insight into the ancient history of the bay, with several fossilized animal remains inside the narrow chamber. Tour guides can point out where the fossils are.

Farther afield on Dau Be Island, Ho Ba Ham, or Three-Tunnel Lake, is another seldom-visited spot that is sometimes included on tours stopping at Cat Ba. As the name suggests, its peaceful, walled-in lagoons are accessed by a series of tunnels, usually in wooden boats at low tide.

Titov Island

Named after Soviet cosmonaut Gherman Titov, the second man to orbit the Earth, Titov Island (Dao Ti Top) (8:30am-5pm daily) was christened after a 1962 visit by the man himself, in which Titov and his host, Ho Chi Minh, admired Ha Long's scenery from this island's very shores. The island's small stretch of white-sand beach, a rarity in the bay, is slightly grubby but manages to attract a fair number of visitors. The volleyball net and beach chairs for rent—not to mention the view—help, and swimming is a popular activity during the warmer months. Titov's best asset is its hilltop lookout, the reward at the end of a zigzagging maze of 427 stone steps. While you may have to catch your breath once or twice en route to the summit, views at the top are the best in the bay and many a photo op takes place here, making it a highlight of Ha Long's more frequented attractions.

Other Sights

Stippled with miniature islands and solitary rock formations, some teetering upon no more than a few feet of limestone at their base, Ha Long has a host of iconic locales. The Incense Burner is a miniature karst standing just off the western side of Dau Go Island. It resembles the incense urns that appear outside local pagodas. It's also featured on Vietnam's VND200,000 note. Farther along, Dog Rock and Ga Choi, also known as Fighting Cock Island, are equally notable landmarks. These formations are large enough to see from the boat, making for good photos. They are only pointed out in passing, so you'll need to pay attention to catch sight of them.

Cruises

Most travelers prefer to visit Ha Long Bay by two- or three-day cruise. These excursions can be regimented, packing many sights and activities into a short time. Spending a night on the water not only affords you more time to explore the bay but also makes the experience memorable. These all-inclusive cruises eliminate much of the hassle involved in traveling to Ha Long, arranging a boat, and setting fees with a local provider. Accommodations run the gamut from dilapidated wooden junks to lavish luxury cruise liners.

Negotiating with budget tour providers is a must. Overnights on the lower end of the spectrum begin at VND1,680,000 per person for a two-day, one-night cruise. These are often disappointing, and anything lower than that price is likely downright dangerous, as not all boats are properly maintained or inspected on a regular basis. The companies listed in this section have solid reputations for providing safe, affordable, and enjoyable cruises, but there are also dozens of other well-known operators in the area. All listed prices are quoted per person for a double-occupancy cabin; if you're traveling solo, you will likely be required to pay an additional single supplement.

While everything from entrance fees to meals and accommodation is included in the package price, you will, in most instances, be expected to pay for your own beverages, which are usually marked up to a few times the going rate on land. It has become a recent trend to sneak beverages onto boats in an attempt to avoid these fees, but the boat crew does not take kindly to this practice.

Some higher-end companies provide day

trips to the bay, but with a four-hour drive to and from Hanoi, it's hardly worth the effort.

BUDGET

One of the more reliable budget providers, **Halong Fantasea Cruises** (office 71B6 Hang Trong, Hanoi, tel. 04/3938-0529, www. halongfantaseacruise.com, 7:30am-8pm daily, VND903,000/one-day, VND1,995,000-2,205,000/two-day, VND3,255,000-3,465,000/ three-day) executes well-run excursions to the bay that save money and are safe and organized. Both deluxe and superior rooms are available, though deluxe offerings tend to be closer to the engine and therefore more prone to noise and a scent of gasoline. A handful of complimentary drinks are included on the trip, though others come with a marked-up price tag. All of Ha Long's most popular sights make the itinerary, including Titov Island and Sung Sot Cave. Daily swimming opportunities and scheduled kayak outings are offered. The three-day tours also stop on Cat Ba Island. Dietary exceptions can be made for vegetarians and those with other restrictions, provided you inform the company ahead of time. The company's booking agents tend to be more straightforward than some of their counterparts, offering honest information on

the state of the boat, rooms, and other necessary details.

MID-RANGE

Glory Cruises (office 5/33B Pham Ngu Lao, Hanoi, tel. 04/3927-5797, www.ha-longglorycruise.com, 9am-5pm Mon.-Fri., 9am-3pm Sat.-Sun., VND2,625,000/one-day, VND3,360,000-3,990,000/two-day, VND5,565,000-6,195,000/three-day) provides a pleasant combination of friendly staff, knowledgeable tour guides, and staterooms for single- and multi-day cruises of the bay. Visit Sung Sot Cave, less-frequented spots like Soi Sim Beach and Lan Ha Bay, and a few fishing villages. Activities like swimming, kayaking, and squid fishing are available, as is evening entertainment like board games and playing cards.

The chic and well-appointed **Pelican Cruises** (office 96 Hang Bac, Hanoi, tel. 04/3933-6222, www.halongpelicancruise. com, 7:30am-5:30pm daily, VND1,785,000/ one-day, VND3,465,000-4,830,000/two-day, VND5,628,000-8,715,000/three-day) operates a small fleet of plush high-end junk boats that ferry travelers to some of Ha Long's more famous attractions as well as a few less-frequented ones. Pelican's cabins are

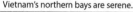

Vietnam's northern bays are serene.

exceptionally well-kept, with modern bathrooms, enclosed showers, and large, comfy beds. Three-day excursions make it out to Lan Ha Bay and its more peaceful surroundings, and activities like swimming and kayaking are included in several itineraries. Ground transportation is not part of the price, with the exception of the one-day trip, though a shuttle bus (VND525,000 round-trip) is available.

The local arm of a century-old American brand, Gray Line Cruises (office 125 Hong Ha Bldg., Hanoi, tel. 04/3717-3229, www.graylinehalong.com, 8am-5:30pm daily, VND945,000/one-day, VND3,885,000-5,145,000/two-day, VND6,510,000-8,610,000/three-day) has been cruising Ha Long since 2013, with modern boats and experienced local guides. The outfit offers one-, two-, and three-day cruises to some of Ha Long's more famous sights as well as Lan Ha Bay, Cat Ba, and the outer edge of Bai Tu Long. Activities like kayaking, swimming, cycling on Cat Ba, and squid fishing are included in some itineraries, and additional snorkeling and diving excursions can be purchased upon request. Transportation to and from Hanoi is not included in the price, though you can hop on the company shuttle bus for a price.

LUXURY

As the only cruise provider fully authorized to venture from Ha Long into neighboring Bai Tu Long Bay, Indochina Junk (office 58 Au Trieu, Hanoi, tel. 04/3926-4085, www.indochina-junk.com, 8am-6pm daily, VND3,510,000/two-day, VND5,670,000/three-day) escapes the well-traveled routes of Ha Long. A series of two- and three-day tours ply the waters east of Vung Vieng floating village, trading the heavy traffic of Ha Long's caves for a quieter cruise to the equally stunning karsts of Bai Tu Long. Better still are the company's efforts to conserve the bay's natural beauty, spearheading a program known as "For a Green Ha Long Bay," which aims to spread the benefits of tourism to local fishermen and communities, organizes clean-up efforts in the bay, and raises awareness about environmental protection within Ha Long's busy waters. All of Indochina Junk's boats are built as traditional Chinese-style junks and include beautiful, well-appointed rooms with air-conditioning, making this a luxury option at mid-range prices.

One of the bay's more well-known operators, Bhaya Cruises (office 47 Phan Chu Trinh, Hanoi, tel. 04/3944-6777, www.bhayacruises.com, 9am-6pm daily, VND3,150,000/one-day, VND3,969,000-7,665,000/two-day, VND7,665,000-15,120,000/three-day) runs a three-vessel fleet of high-end boats that are replicas of emperor Khai Dinh's famous wooden ship. Multi-day cruises ply the waters between Ha Long, Cat Ba Island, and the outer edge of Bai Tu Long, with stops at a combination of much-visited and off-the-beaten-path attractions. Swimming and kayaking at Vung Ha Beach and guided cycling tours of Cat Ba feature on some itineraries. Transportation to and from Hanoi (shuttle VND630,000/group, private car VND4,515,000/group) is not included in the cost.

Also operated by Bhaya, Au Co Cruises (office 47 Phan Chu Trinh, Hanoi, tel. 04/3933-4545, www.aucocruises.com, 9:30am-6pm daily, VND4,179,000/one-day, VND8,295,000/two-day, VND11,760,000-20,200,000/three-day) is the more luxurious offshoot of its parent company. Their vessel, The Au Co, has swanky cabins, with bamboo and sliding glass doors, enclosed showers, and chic design accents. They have a high-end restaurant onboard, making for a posh environment. The one-day cruises are not as worthwhile as the three-day outings, which tour Ha Long, Bai Tu Long, and Cat Ba, and include leisurely activities, such as kayaking at Vung Ha Beach and cycling tours at Cat Ba.

Transportation

The majority of overnight tours include transportation to and from Hanoi in their price. For those making their own way to Ha Long City, booking agents and travel outfits in Hanoi can arrange minibus transport to the city for around VND130,000 per person. The trip takes around four hours and usually includes a stop at an overpriced souvenir outlet somewhere along the way.

Many cruise operators provide a shuttle bus or private car option, but these are far more expensive, with shuttle buses running VND525,000-630,000 per group and private cars costing at least VND4,000,000 per group.

Local buses travel from Luong Yen bus station (3 Nguyen Khoai, tel. 04/3927-0477) in Hanoi to Bai Chay bus station (near corner of Le Huu Trac and QL18, tel. 03/3364-9230) in Ha Long City. At VND100,000 a head, you're better off arranging tourist transport, as this saves you the additional cost of getting to and from these bus stations, not to mention navigating the bus system.

Most vessels cast off from Bai Chay Pier (Ha Long, tel. 03/3384-6592, www.benxe-bentauquangninh.vn, 6:30am-4:30pm daily), Ha Long City's tourist hub. High-end cruises usually depart farther west from Tuan Chau Island (Tuan Chau Island, tel. 03/3655-0009, www.tuanchau-halong.com.vn), about seven miles west of Bai Chay Pier. A select few leave from Hon Gai Pier (6A Le Thanh Tong), closer to Ha Long City's center. Even those who travel independently to Ha Long City should be in contact with the tour provider to get detailed directions to the correct pier.

BAI TU LONG BAY

Legend puts the home of Mother Dragon in Ha Long Bay; her children are just next door in Bai Tu Long, a cloudy aquamarine expanse dotted with the same limestone karsts, mysterious caves, and lush greenery. Separated by an invisible border a few miles east of the city, this nearby, smaller bay has long played second fiddle to its more famous neighbor but is fast gaining favor among foreign visitors for its less-crowded waters away from the heavy traffic of Ha Long. Local residents live amid its gravity-defying islands and larger-than-life landscapes.

While it is possible to reach the bay's Quan Lan Island on your own, tours of Bai Tu Long are only available through one outfitter, Indochina Junk.

Vung Vieng Fishing Village

Easily Bai Tu Long's most-visited sight, Vung Vieng is one of the bay's fishing communities, comprised of a modest collection of floating houses. Residents live 15 miles offshore, in the shadow of soaring limestone karsts, taking shelter in small, buoyant dwellings that are clustered together on Bai Tu Long's placid waters. Local fishers row visitors to village sights, like the schoolhouse and a few residents' homes, for a taste of daily life in Vung Vieng.

Thien Canh Son Cave

Thien Canh Son Cave is the most impressive of Bai Tu Long's caverns, a vast chamber of sparkling stalactites and unusual formations that is lit by just a few standard light bulbs, retaining the cave's natural atmosphere and beauty. It takes 30-45 minutes to tour the expansive interior.

In the evenings, this eerie cavern occasionally becomes a dining room thanks to Indochina Junk, which runs a three-day, two-night tour in which guests can enjoy a meal within the hollows.

Quan Lan Island

Once an 11th-century trading port, Quan Lan Island is among a handful of islands in Bai Tu Long inhabited by locals that is now slowly beginning to reap the benefits of tourism. This long, narrow stretch of rock sits on the southern border of the bay, facing away from the mainland toward the stunning Gulf of Tonkin, an hour-long ferry ride from shore, and boasts some of the most secluded beaches in Vietnam. Once you've reached the island, there isn't much to do beyond admire the scenery. Its sleepy village and unbeatable views are enough to attract at least a few visitors and to get local authorities to seriously consider how best to develop the area for foreign visitors.

Transportation

TOURS

Thanks to a fair amount of guidebook hype and growing tourist interest, more than a few tour providers list the bay in their travel programs. Indochina Junk (58 Au Trieu, tel. 04/3926-4085, www.indochina-junk.com, 8am-6pm daily, VND3,510,000/two-day, VND5,670,000/three-day) is the only outfitter approved by local authorities to enter Bai Tu Long's waters. Indochina Junk's tours go all the way to Thien Canh Son Cave, Cap La Island, and the bay's Cong Dam area. All other agencies that include a trip to Bai Tu Long simply touch upon the border of the two bays, stopping over at Vung Vieng fishing village.

FERRIES TO QUAN LAN ISLAND

Independent travelers can overnight on largely undeveloped Quan Lan Island. Daily high-speed ferries (tel. 03/3247-3536, 7:30am and 2pm daily, VND120,000) depart from Cai Rong Port, just over 30 miles east of Ha Long City, returning to the mainland at 2:30pm. Local buses from Hanoi make the trip to Cua Ong Market, not far from the port, and from there tourists hop on a boat to Quan Lan.

Once you arrive, there is little to do on the island other than wander and enjoy the view. A handful of guesthouses in the main town offer overnight accommodations. Expect little to no English and limited dining options. Nicer hotels run VND500,000-700,000 per night, with cheaper guesthouses costing around VND150,000-200,000 per night. Amenities will be no more than running water and a fan at the cheaper places, and perhaps an air-conditioner in the nicer hotels, with the potential for hot water. Book ahead of time to ensure there's a room available, though you may need to enlist a Vietnamese speaker, or book through a local travel agency.

CAT BA ISLAND

You would never know how popular Ha Long Bay is from a visit to Cat Ba National Park, surrounded by nothing but nature, or while plying the placid waters of nearby Lan Ha Bay. From Cat Ba Island, you'll enjoy a quieter and more independent version of Ha Long, escaping the heavy traffic of the larger bay's tourist boats. Cat Ba's main town is an unattractive jumble of cookie-cutter hotels and travel agencies, but beyond the main drag is plenty of hiking, cycling, kayaking, and climbing amid the incredible coastline of northern Vietnam.

Cat Ba's wild and wonderful national park is a real must-see, and includes hiking and trekking. Equally appealing are the waters of Lan Ha Bay, a smaller, quieter version of its northern cousin, Ha Long. Lan Ha can be enjoyed on a basic boat tour, scaling the limestone karsts of the bay on a rock-climbing outing, or kayaking through eroded tunnels to one of the bay's 100-plus beaches.

Though it can be gloomy in the off season, particularly as the north's signature mist drifts in and obscures the island's beautiful views, Cat Ba has something to offer even in poor weather. The eerie winter fog is pleasant company compared to the droves of visitors the island receives June-August, when Vietnamese tourists are on holiday.

Getting to Cat Ba requires extra effort, but the rewards are more than worth the work. A growing number of tour companies include stopovers on Cat Ba during their three-day itineraries, but these will only give you an overnight (at most) on the island.

With the exception of Hospital Cave, Cannon Fort, and the Cat Co beaches, most sights in Cat Ba require a guide in order to visit. Much of the island is remote and is most safely enjoyed with a knowledgeable local.

★ Cat Ba National Park

Legend has it that the rugged limestone mountains and winding underground caverns of Cat Ba National Park (Vuon Quoc Gia Cat Ba) (tel. 03/1368-8981, www.vuonquocgiacatba.com.vn, 7am-4pm daily, VND15,000-35,000) came about after a dragon tumbled into the sea, denting the island's terrain with

Cat Ba Island

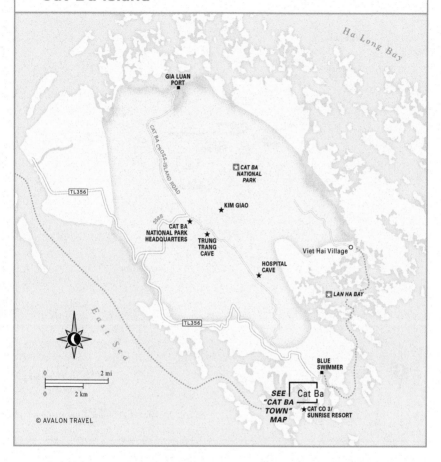

its tail. These rolling hills and rutted formations on the northeastern part of the island provide a habitat for civets, leopards, giant squirrels, dozens of stunning bird species, and over 1,500 varieties of plants, as well as the Cat Ba langur, among the most endangered primates in the world.

A handful of relatively untouched trails wind through the heart of Cat Ba. Most trails range from moderate to strenuous and meander deep into the jungle. On the bay, activities like rock-climbing are available on a few islands, as is swimming, kayaking, and boating.

On most adventures, a guide is necessary to show you the ropes.

TRUNG TRANG CAVE
One of the park's highlights is **Trung Trang Cave** (VND15,000, plus VND70,000/guide), an underground passageway that lies just up the road from Hospital Cave before the park's head office. Discovered in 1938, this cavern winds 984 feet through the base of a limestone karst and was used in the early 1960s as a hideout for members of the Vietnamese navy. Inside the cave, the small, meandering

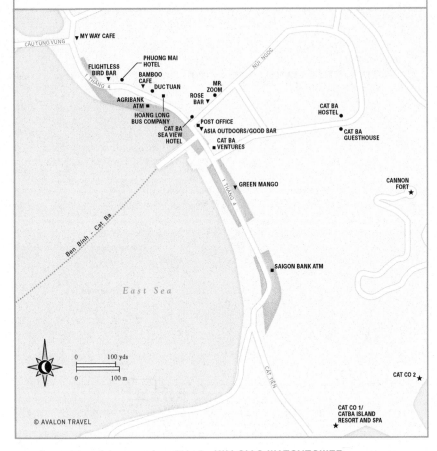

Cat Ba Town

MY WAY CAFE

CẦU TÙNG VŨNG

NÚI NGỌC

FLIGHTLESS BIRD BAR

PHUONG MAI HOTEL

BAMBOO CAFE

1 THÁNG 4

DUC TUAN

MR. ZOOM

ROSE BAR

AGRIBANK ATM

HOANG LONG BUS COMPANY

CAT BA SEA VIEW HOTEL

POST OFFICE

ASIA OUTDOORS/GOOD BAR

CAT BA VENTURES

CAT BA HOSTEL

CAT BA GUESTHOUSE

Ben Binh - Cat Ba

1 THÁNG 4

GREEN MANGO

CANNON FORT ★

East Sea

SAIGON BANK ATM

0   100 yds
0   100 m

CAT TIEN

CAT CO 2 ★

CAT CO 1/ CATBA ISLAND RESORT AND SPA ★

© AVALON TRAVEL

tunnel transitions from smooth, polished walls to spindly stalactites to barnacle-like growths wallpapered against its interior, which is home to scores of tiny bats who nap overhead.

Guides don't speak much English, but they'll point out several formations, some of which resemble elephants, birds, or Buddhas; one or two of these require some imagination. Be prepared to crouch down, as the cavern has low ceilings in some places. Before entering Trung Trang, head past the cave to the national park headquarters to buy an entry ticket and link up with one of the required guides.

KIM GIAO WATCHTOWER

On a clear day, the Kim Giao Watchtower (VND15,000) boasts some of the best views on the island. To get there, it's a moderate hike up to the mountain's summit. The two-hour out-and-back journey (just over a half-mile each way) begins at the park's headquarters on a paved route that turns into a well-trodden dirt path, which then becomes stone steps on the ascent. The path zigzags up to a small lookout, where you can take in a panoramic view of the park.

Guides (VND100,000) can be arranged either directly from the park or through one of the tour operators in town as a half-day excursion.

TREK TO VIET HAI VILLAGE

The most challenging trek in the park is to Viet Hai Village (VND35,000, plus VND500,000/guide), a nine-mile, four- to five-hour journey. The hike rambles up massive limestone boulders and over five different jungle peaks before sliding into a peaceful farming village on the eastern side of the island. This is one of the best excursions Cat Ba has to offer. If you're lucky, you might catch a rare glimpse of wild macaques and even the Cat Ba langur.

Though the route begins as a tame, paved road from the national park headquarters, it soon deteriorates into limestone boulders to scramble over and, later, a narrow dirt path that winds its way through some of the island's most untouched areas. Two or three miles in, the hike passes by Frog Lake, which is no more than an oversized puddle. Upon reaching Viet Hai Village, you will have an easy seaside walk to the port, where a slow boat floats you back to town.

Substantial footwear is a must, as are long pants. Mosquito protection is not a bad idea, and you'll probably want to bring a backpack or something that keeps your hands free, as the latter part of the descent into Viet Hai Village has you scrambling over rocks.

Tours still run on rainy days and can be just as fun, though the wetter the trail gets the more treacherous it becomes. Most guides are highly experienced and do a good job of keeping you safe, but some of the more challenging passes can still be dangerous for less-confident hikers. This is a difficult hike on a normal day; it's very difficult on a rainy day.

While the national park provides travelers with all the tools required to do this trek, it's more cost-effective to hop on a tour from town. To do the trek independently, it costs VND35,000 for the park entry, VND500,000 for the required guide, and an additional VND500,000 to hire a boat from Viet Hai back to Cat Ba Town. For a full-day excursion through one of the local tour providers, the going rate is around VND380,000 per person and includes both lunch and transportation to and from Cat Ba.

Hospital Cave

A popular stop en route to Cat Ba National Park, Hospital Cave (Hang Quan Y) (8am-5pm daily, VND15,000) was used as a medical facility, shelter, and strategy base for north Vietnamese forces during the American War. Alongside their Chinese allies, Communist soldiers constructed a three-story complex inside the massive cave from 1963 to 1965 with 17 rooms, including patient beds, an operating theater, a meeting hall, a cinema, and several other facilities. The first floor, made entirely of concrete, was where most operations took place and boasts incredible acoustics—one person's voice will reverberate throughout the entire floor. The second-floor space, where films were sometimes played, provides more natural surroundings, with vaulted limestone ceilings. The cave could house 200 people at any given time during the war. Though bombs were dropped around this site, nothing inside the cavern was ever damaged by American attacks, as this particular cave remained undetected throughout the war.

When visiting Hospital Cave, your only option is to park across the street at a small roadside café, where entry tickets are sold. It's not required, but you're better off hiring the sole on-site guide (VND30,000), an outgoing man by the name of Mr. Cuong who is knowledgeable and well versed in the history of the place, bringing to life the war within these bare concrete rooms. Afterward, the café across the street is a nice spot for a drink and the owners are a friendly crowd.

Cannon Fort

On a clear day, the view from Cannon Fort (Phao Dai Than Cong, tel. 03/1388-8686, 7am-5pm daily, VND50,000) is one of the best on the island. Built by the French in 1942, this 20th-century military lookout was used to protect the city of Haiphong from attack during the Franco-Vietnam War, and later used during the Japanese occupation and the American conflict. Three sides of the island are visible from the top of this 580-foot hill, including some stunning views of the fishing port and the bay, and you'll be able to catch a glimpse of the two hilltop cannons for which the place is named. There is a small exhibition room located in one of the bunkers, though it lacks signage. In all, the main reason for a visit here is the view, so make this trip only on a clear day.

The road leading to Cannon Fort begins in Cat Ba Town. There is a sign at the bottom of the hill directing visitors to the fort.

Cat Co Beaches

A short walk from Cat Ba town, the trio of Cat Co beaches, snuggled into many coves on the southeastern tip of the island, are worth a visit during warm weather. There are resorts located right on the water, which regulate access to the beaches, particularly Cat Co 2 and 3. In order to spend time on the beach, you're expected to purchase a drink or meal from the resort, but you don't need to be staying at a resort.

Cat Co 1 is a more local affair and the most easily accessible of the beaches. It's where Cat Ba Island Resort and Spa (Cat Co 1, tel. 03/1368-8686, www.catbaislandresort-spa.com) has set up a water park (6am-6pm daily, VND200,000) along the shore that is popular with Vietnamese tourists during the summer. The park is virtually a ghost town in the off season. During November and December, it's often possible to access Cat Co 1 for free.

From the main road, hang a left and you'll come to the Cat Ba Beach Resort (Cat Co 2, tel. 03/1388-8686, www.catbabeachresort. com, 6am-10pm daily) on Cat Co 2.

A pretty cliffside path from Cat Co 1 leads around to the Cat Ba Sunrise Resort (Cat Co 3, tel. 03/1388-7360, www.catbasunriseresort.com, 7am-8pm daily) on Cat Co 3, a quieter stretch of sand where resort guests and outside visitors can come and soak up the sun. Of the three resorts, this is the only one worth staying at overnight.

★ Lan Ha Bay

In the small, quiet Lan Ha Bay, located off Cat Ba's eastern shores, trademark limestone karsts rise sharply out of the sea. Dotted with roughly 400 islands, over 100 miniature white-sand beaches, and a secluded fishing village here and there, the bay is a popular

Kayaks are a popular way to explore Lan Ha Bay.

Good Bar

(Ben Beo, tel. 03/1368-8237, www.blueswim-mersailing.com, 8am-10pm daily) also offers kayaking tours.

Tours

Nearly every hotel, restaurant, and guesthouse on 1 Thang 4 offers standard excursions to the national park and the island's surrounding bays.

Half- and full-day guided jungle treks to the national park are available for as little as VND350,000 per person. For the best value, shop around along the harborfront. The folks at Cat Ba Ventures (223 1 Thang 4, tel. 09/1246-7016, www.catbaventures.com, 7:30am-8pm daily) are a good choice for both trekking and boat tours, though they only seem eager to offer a helping hand after you've forked over your cash.

Nightlife

Cat Ba doesn't offer much in the way of night-life, but you'll find a few casual hangouts stretched along the harborfront. Most places close up shop by around 10pm, though there are one or two bars that will stay open until the last customer leaves.

Outfitted with retro polka dot couches and a whole host of Kiwi paraphernalia, the Flightless Bird Bar (189 1 Thang 4, tel. 03/1388-8517, 10am-last customer daily, VND20,000-80,000) serves drinks only and is a pleasant spot for a late afternoon beverage or some sound travel advice. The cozy indoor room plays a selection of Western music and the bar is stocked with beer and both Vietnamese and Western spirits as well as the occasional bottle of wine. This is also, inexplicably, the place to go for a foot or head massage, or a manicure, as these services are cheap (most under VND60,000) and can be combined with your happy hour.

The liveliest nighttime hangout in Cat Ba town, Good Bar (Noble House, 222 1 Thang 4, tel. 03/1388-8363, 7am-10:30pm downstairs, 2am upstairs daily, VND20,000-100,000) slings cold beers, cocktails, spirits, and some pretty average Western food downstairs in its

venue for kayaking, sailing, and deep-water soloing excursions, in addition to standard boat cruises. Lan Ha gets busy in the summer months, when domestic tourists hit the island, but with so many travelers opting for a trip to nearby Ha Long over the bay, this is a far more serene and authentic option.

Lan Ha is experienced via boat tour from Cat Ba Island. Prices for boat tours begin around VND550,000 for a full-day outing to Lan Ha Bay with a brief stop at one or two of Ha Long's most famous sights. These are a popular option, though read the itinerary before signing up; some outings are advertised as day tours of Ha Long when, in reality, boats tend to stick to Lan Ha and only make a quick jaunt into the larger bay.

One boat tour outfitter is Cat Ba Ventures (223 1 Thang 4, tel. 09/1246-7016, www.cat-baventures.com, 7:30am-8pm daily). Another, Asia Outdoors (Noble House, 2nd Fl., 222 1 Thang 4, tel. 03/1368-8450, www.asiaout-doors.com.vn, 8am-8pm daily), offers rock-climbing and kayaking trips. Blue Swimmer ground-floor restaurant and two stories up, past the Asia Outdoors office, where the setting is reminiscent of a bar, complete with pool and foosball tables, a wide balcony overlooking the harbor, and a good music selection. Happy hour specials and regular drink deals are offered, though most only apply to the upper level and not the downstairs restaurant-style seating area. Confirm with your server to avoid surprises on the bill.

The hole-in-the-wall **Rose Bar** (15 Nui Ngoc, tel. 03/1388-8472, catbarosebar@gmail. com, 5pm-late daily, VND15,000-115,000) just off the main drag is a slightly cramped and heavily graffitied bar room that boasts a dart board, pool table, foosball, and other games. The menu matches that of most similar businesses in town, with beer, cocktails, and spirits on offer at good prices, and draws a fair number of thirsty patrons throughout the night. If you're dying to hear your own playlist, patrons are allowed to hook their own iPods into the bar's sound system for a people's choice music selection.

Sports and Recreation

With the incredible outdoors so close to town, the wild and wonderful Cat Ba has fast developed into Vietnam's best-known adventure tourism hub. Activities like cycling, climbing, trekking, and kayaking are popular here and can be arranged through most tour companies in town. Sand flies are present at the beaches; repellent can be a big help with this. Most tour outfits have their own repellent for guest use, but check beforehand.

CYCLING

The only place to offer quality mountain bikes for exploring the island is **Blue Swimmer** (Ben Beo, tel. 03/1368-8237, www. blueswimmersailing.com, 8am-10pm daily, VND315,000/day), located beside the harbor in Lan Ha Bay about five minutes from town. All bikes are imported Treks, which helps to justify the high price, and they can be brought to your hotel if requested. Guided day trips are available for an additional fee, and the

company has a few sample itineraries listed on its website for those interested in blazing their own trails.

ROCK CLIMBING

Easily the best location for rock climbing in Vietnam, Cat Ba and its infinite limestone mountains are a perfect place to get started as a beginner or flex your climbing muscles as a seasoned pro. Whether on a beach in Lan Ha Bay or deep within Butterfly Valley, the island offers more than enough opportunity to scale its many rock faces. For experienced climbers, deep-water soloing is an option, affording those keen on seeing the bay with a more challenging way to climb. **Asia Outdoors** (Noble House, 2nd Fl., 222 1 Thang 4, tel. 03/1368-8450, www.asiaoutdoors.com.vn, 8am-8pm daily), Cat Ba's first and only certified climbing outfit, runs daily trips (VND1,722,000 per person) to its beachfront climbing space in Lan Ha Bay combined with a bit of kayaking. They can also tailor trips to a traveler's individual requests. Staff are fun, friendly, and knowledgeable in both climbing and the area. For more information, stop by the office and chat with the staff or pick up a copy of Asia Outdoors' climbing guidebook for Vietnam.

KAYAKING

Lan Ha's soaring cliffs and peaceful waters are best explored by kayak. Paddle your way across open channels and into small, secluded lagoons; sidle up beside a towering rock face; or float your way through the eroded arches that sit beneath the bay's gravity-defying islands. Dozens of travel outfits in Cat Ba town offer kayaking excursions around Lan Ha at varying rates. When booking, clarify whether or not you'll have a guide paddling along with you and exactly how much time you'll have to explore. The folks at **Blue Swimmer** (Ben Beo, tel. 03/1368-8237, www.blueswimmersailing.com, 8am-10pm daily, VND315,000/day) offer daily rentals as well as a test paddle if you're not sure but want to give it a try.

Saving Cat Ba's Langurs

It's rare to spot a Cat Ba langur, one of the world's most endangered primates, swinging through the trees of the island's national park. These small, golden-headed creatures are native only to Cat Ba Island, and decades of poaching have reduced their numbers from approximately 2,500 in the 1960s to somewhere between 60 and 70 today. Hunted almost exclusively as an ingredient in traditional Chinese medicine, the langur's population reached rock-bottom in 2000, with only 53 animals remaining in the wild.

Thanks to the efforts of a number of German conservation groups, including the Muenster Zoo and the Frankfurt Zoological Society, the fate of the langur is looking up. The Cat Ba Langur Conservation Project (www.catbalangur.org) helps monitor preservation efforts, which protect the natural habitat of seven small sub-populations within Cat Ba National Park who use caves for shelter and survive mostly on flowers, shoots, and leaves. Only three of the seven groups are able to reproduce, further challenging the future of the species. Local communities have become involved in the protection endeavors and Cat Ba's langur is now considered a symbol of the island. For more information, check the Conservation Project's website.

TREKKING

With the vast majority of Cat Ba covered in dense jungle, trekking opportunities abound here, both in and around the national park. For a venture farther off the beaten track, excursions in Butterfly Valley and around Lien Minh, one of the oldest villages on the island, offer more scrambling over rocks and up hills. Guides are required on all trips and can be hired via the national park or booked through a tour in town. To hike to Viet Hai via Frog Lake in Cat Ba National Park, jump on a tour from town to save some money. Tour operators also do this same journey, including a hike up to Kim Giao watchtower, but **Asia Outdoors** (Noble House, 2nd Fl., 222 1 Thang 4, tel. 03/1368-8450, www.asiaoutdoors.com.vn, 8am-8pm daily) is really the only one to venture into Butterfly Valley.

Accommodations

Hotels on Cat Ba are multiplying at a breakneck pace, with a new construction job starting every other day. You'll find tons of hotels along 1 Thang 4, with rooms that offer excellent views of the harbor at slightly higher but still-reasonable prices. The hostels and guesthouses tucked down Nui Ngoc and farther from the water go for much less. In the off season, private beds can be had for as little as VND60,000 a night, though many hoteliers also work as tour guides or travel agents and so these accommodations are usually accompanied by a big push for tours and additional services. Few hotels on the island offer an included breakfast that is actually worth the price tag. Don't expect too much out of your hotel's wireless connection, as there is usually a single router placed on the ground floor that is weak at best. Hoteliers on the island have taken to keeping the "on" switch for the water heater downstairs at reception, so expect to ask for your hot shower beforehand.

The summer months are especially hectic on Cat Ba. If you're dying to grab a waterfront spot or have a particular hotel in mind, make your reservation 1-2 weeks ahead of time. During the rest of the year, hotels have many vacancies, so you can book a room the day of. Listed rates are based on the high season for foreign tourists (Nov.-Dec.), rather than the Vietnamese high season (June-Aug.), when the island is at its busiest and prices are highest. Verify rates beforehand if you plan to visit June-August.

UNDER VND210,000

At the top of Nui Ngoc away from the harbor, **Cat Ba Hostel** (160 Nui Ngoc, tel. 09/7789-4883, www.catbahostel.com, VND60,000 dorm, VND160,000 double) is a worthy choice for budget travelers, with unbeatable prices and clean, well-kept accommodations to match. Hot water, air-conditioning, TV, and Wi-Fi are featured in all rooms, and you'll find personal lockers in the dorms, as well as en suite bathrooms. Downstairs, the hostel runs a travel outfit and can offer advice on the surrounding area.

Directly opposite Cat Ba Hostel, Cat Ba Guesthouse (227 Nui Ngoc, tel. 09/0600-0227, VND60,000 dorm, VND120,000 double) may not have the same additional services to offer, but its accommodations are just as good as the competition, with hot water, air-conditioning, TV, and Wi-Fi access throughout the building. Five-bed dorms include a communal balcony and en suite bathroom, while doubles are a little older but still great for the price.

Dirt-cheap and clean, Mr. Zoom Backpacker Hostel (25 Nui Ngoc, tel. 03/1369-6230, VND80,000-210,000) is tucked just off the harbor-front road and offers no-frills accommodations for the backpacker crowd. Rooms include hot water, air-conditioning, and semi-hard beds. The owner speaks English well and can arrange tours and various excursions around the island. Note, there is a karaoke bar nearby that gets active during the evenings, though it never stays open too late.

Right in the middle of 1 Thang 4 street, the Cat Ba Sea View (220 1 Thang 4, tel. 03/1388-8201, www.catbaseaviewhotel.com, VND160,000-250,000) is the nicest of the island's harbor-front accommodations and boasts a notably friendly staff to go with its tidy, well-kept rooms. Amenities include television and Wi-Fi access, hot water, air-conditioning, plush duvet covers, and a fridge. Beautiful views of the harbor are available on the street-facing side of the hotel, while rooms at the back provide equally good value accommodations without the window. There is a small restaurant and café downstairs.

VND210,000-525,000

Right in the center of town, rooms at the Phuong Mai (193 1 Thang 4, tel. 09/1461-8308, VND210,000-250,000) are on par with most other accommodations along this street. The amiable owner, Mr. Khanh, and his family go a long way to make the experience unique. Mr. Khanh can help with advice on the island. Rooms come with hot water, Wi-Fi access, air-conditioning, and TV, not to mention some nice views of the harbor. The first two stories of the building serve as a hair salon.

The Duc Tuan Hotel (210 1 Thang 4, tel. 03/1388-8783, www.ductuancatbahotel.com, VND210,000-315,000) offers clean, well-appointed rooms, many of which come with a nice harbor-front view. Amenities include air-conditioning, hot water, touch-and-go Wi-Fi access, TV, a minibar, an in-room safe, and tea- and coffee-making facilities. Mattresses are a little hard but not the worst on the island. Downstairs, you'll find that the hotel operates a restaurant and a tour-booking agency out of the ground floor, in addition to renting out motorbikes and bicycles. Breakfast is included in the room rate, but it is also possible to opt out of this, if preferred. Prices dip as low as VND210,000 in winter.

VND1,050,000-2,100,000

The finest of the lot on Cat Ba, Sunrise Resort (Cat Co 3, tel. 03/1388-7360, www.catbasunriseresort.com, VND1,800,000-4,600,000) is nestled away in the peaceful cove of Cat Co 3 beach, far enough removed from town to avoid the tourist trail but still well within walking distance. As the only property on the beach, its spacious, modern rooms feature the height of local luxury, including television, Wi-Fi access, a minibar, hot water, air-conditioning, tea- and coffee-making facilities, an in-room safety box, and the best sea views on the island. More posh accommodations also throw in a balcony, and all guests are free to enjoy a complimentary breakfast, as well as use of the beach out front. Restaurant and massage services are available on site, though additional services tend to be overpriced.

Food

Most of the fare on the island is bland, with every harbor-front hotel offering a similar menu of standard but overpriced backpacker grub. For cheaper options, head inland up Nui Ngoc. Wherever you eat, don't expect to be wowed: this is not the place to revel in the tastes of Vietnamese cuisine. For snacks and other necessities, you can also swing by the cache of convenience stores off the main road on Nui Ngoc south of the main harbor.

Completely outfitted in its namesake, the Bamboo Cafe (1 Thang 4, tel. 03/1388-7552, 7am-9:30pm daily, VND40,000-145,000) offers a decent mix of Western and Vietnamese dishes at reasonable prices, not to mention some of the better service in town. Owned by a former tour guide, the restaurant serves average meals in addition to offering useful travel advice. The rest of the family, who staff the eatery, are equally amiable and willing to help.

For your European caffeine fix, My Way Cafe (164C 1 Thang 4, 7am-10pm daily, VND15,000-70,000) makes the best lattes, cappuccinos, and coffee-related beverages on the island and also offers happy hour specials on its alcoholic drinks, most of which are less than VND110,000. Solid Vietnamese offerings are served, though service can be slow at times.

You'll find the best dining on Cat Ba at Green Mango (1 Thang 4, tel. 03/1388-7151, www.greenmango.vn, 7am-7pm daily, VND80,000-470,000), a white-tablecloth place that is well-priced for its offerings, which include Western breakfasts, pizzas, and other dishes. Both indoor and outdoor seating is available, with the latter facing the harbor. The restaurant has inconsistent hours during the low season.

Information and Services

TOURIST INFORMATION

With so many travel and tour agencies attached to hotels, it can be difficult to come across independent information on Cat Ba, as most of these booking offices are not interested in assisting travelers unless they can earn a cut in the process. Asia Outdoors (Noble House, 2nd Fl., 222 1 Thang 4, tel. 03/1368-8450, www.asiaoutdoors.com.vn, 8am-8pm daily) has plenty of useful information on its website and is more than willing to help in person, as are the friendly folks at Flightless Bird Bar (189 1 Thang 4, tel. 03/1388-8517, 10am-last customer daily). You can also ask your hotel for a map, which most hotels are willing to at least loan out to travelers.

BANKS

There is an Agribank ATM (1 Thang 4) located right on the main drag of Cat Ba town as well as a Saigon Bank ATM (1 Thang 4) down the farther end of the harbor. These are the only two ATMs on the island, so bring enough currency. Some hotels may be able to change currency, but make sure the rate isn't too high. If possible, change your money before arriving on the island.

INTERNET AND POSTAL SERVICES

The island's post office (corner of 1 Thang 4 and Nui Ngoc, tel. 03/1388-8569, 8am-noon and 2pm-6pm daily) is often closed during the winter months but sports a letter box outside the building, which is allegedly emptied twice a day. It's probably better to save your mail for your next destination to ensure that it arrives. Most wireless connections on the island are dismal; if Internet is a must, your best bet is to ask your hotel.

MEDICAL SERVICES

There are no real medical facilities on Cat Ba with the exception of the island's sole hospital, a small and often-empty clinic that lies about a mile out of town and is poorly equipped.

For anything that a first-aid kit can't fix, head back to the mainland.

Getting There
FROM HA LONG CITY

A rusted, open-air local **ferry** (Tuan Chau Island, 7:30am, 11:30am, and 3pm daily, VND50,000) runs to Cat Ba Island from the city of Ha Long each day, arriving on the northern side of the island at Gia Luan port. The ferry ride is 35-45 minutes. This point of entry often makes a bad first impression, so it is strongly recommended that you reach the island via Haiphong rather than Ha Long.

As you disembark at Gia Luan port, the usual group of touts will appear, demanding exorbitant rates (VND200,000-800,000) for motorbikes and taxis into Cat Ba town. While such harassment is a common occurrence in Vietnam, this is where things really get ugly. There is a **green local bus** (VND20,000), which runs directly into Cat Ba town. In some cases, the touts turn on the bus drivers when tourists attempt to board the bus, shouting and intimidating them into denying tourists entry or overcharging them.

Some bus drivers lie and attempt to convince tourists that theirs is the local bus, though the correct vehicles are green in color and have a sign saying Cat Ba on the front. If you wait for the correct bus or walk on and ignore the touts and the impostor buses, you will be stalked by touts, now on motorbikes, as they know that you have no other option when heading the 14 miles into town.

All this can make for an unpleasant experience. There are two solutions to this. The first is to simply pay the inflated fare and avoid any confrontation (though this encourages such behavior to continue). Your next best bet is to board the local bus anyway, even if touts are bullying the bus driver into overcharging you. Negotiate the price with the bus fee collector when the touts are out of earshot. It's still possible to be slightly overcharged—VND50,000, for example, instead of VND20,000. The tickets show the fare printed directly on the paper, so you can attempt to contest any overcharging. The bus ride into town is 15-20 minutes.

FROM HAIPHONG

The fastest and most hassle-free way to reach Cat Ba is from Haiphong. Daily **hydrofoil boats** (45-min. ride, VND200,000) depart as early as 7am and run until 3pm, dropping passengers directly in the heart of Cat Ba town. These aging vessels are operated by **Cat Ba Island Resort and Spa** (Cat Co 1, tel. 03/1358-8999, www.catbaislandresort-spa.com). Tickets are sold at the Haiphong dock (4 Ben Binh) and should be purchased ahead of time during summer. The rest of the year, tickets can be purchased at the time of departure. Ticket vendors roam the pier in Haiphong, but not all are honest. Check the resort's website for full details and the correct price, or pop into the (often unstaffed) ticket office, where prices are listed on the wall. There are some independent vendors who sell legitimate tickets, but check that the price is printed on them before purchasing. The boats also run in the opposite direction, with boats departing from the **Fish Harbor** (Cang Ca) opposite 1 Thang 4 street in Cat Ba town at 8am, 10am, 2pm, and 4pm daily.

Bus-boat-bus tickets (VND150,000-200,000) can be purchased from both Haiphong (3.5 hours) and Hanoi. The bus hops on a series of ferries via Cat Hai Island before arriving on Cat Ba and bringing passengers directly into town. When booking your bus ticket, confirm where it lets off. To get back to Haiphong from Cat Ba, the most reliable bus provider on the island is **Hoang Long** (217 1 Thang 4, tel. 03/1388-7224, www.hoanglongasia.com, 7am-5pm daily).

Getting Around
BUSES

If you're not comfortable on a motorbike, the cheapest and easiest way to get to Cat Ba National Park and its many sights is by **local bus** (VND20,000). Minibuses depart from the town center at 8am and follow the road out to the park's headquarters, passing by Hospital Cave. For the return trip, it's just as easy to flag down a minibus heading in the opposite direction in order to get back to town.

TAXIS AND *XE OM*
Motorbike drivers are easily found on the harbor-front street. Should you venture anywhere else (the national park, for example), arrange transportation back ahead of time. Larger vehicles can be hired through your hotel. Taxis are few and far between here.

VEHICLES FOR HIRE
Most hotels and guesthouses around town rent out motorbikes to travelers, starting around VND80,000 for the day. Bicycles are also available, though it's recommended that you opt for the more expensive, high-quality rental if you're planning a cycling day, as the island's hills are not easily tackled on a basic bike. Check the quality of your vehicle before setting off: Cat Ba's less-than-stellar roads can be challenging enough even on a well-maintained vehicle.

HA LONG CITY
Despite the bay's majestic waters and jungle-clad karsts, Ha Long City is a rather underwhelming place. It's best used as a home base from which to do a day cruise of Ha Long Bay, as a substitute for the pricey overnight cruises. Few people stray beyond the droves of hotels and clutch of restaurants lining the main drag, where Bai Chay, Ha Long Bay's most active pier, welcomes countless visitors each day.

Bai Chay
To kill some time in town, take a stroll along Bai Chay Beach, a small beach east of the pier of the same name. There are decent views of the bay's jagged peaks from here, like a mismatched set of teeth spread out along the horizon. Several cafés along this stretch face the water, inviting travelers to come in and relax. Neither the beach nor the water are particularly clean, making this a sightseeing-only spot.

Accommodations
Few travelers stay more than a night or two in Ha Long City. Budget visitors are best off staying close to Bai Chay Pier, where boats depart for Ha Long Bay every morning. Here, a string of cheap and cheerful mini-hotels line the left side of Vuon Dao street, just off the main road.

A few mid-range options dot the main road, but if you're looking to unwind in style, there are posh hotels gathered around Tuan Chau Pier, seven miles west of Bai Chay. The majority of luxury cruise boats depart from Tuan Chau. The only upmarket hotel near Bai Chay is the Novotel.

It's easiest to wait to book a bay tour until you reach Ha Long City. From here, every hotel has its own travel service and it's all but assumed that you'll be using your hotel's tour outfitter for your bay tour. If you book with a different company from your hotel, expect your hotelier to be (at best) a little gruff. It's a good idea to consider the tour offerings and the hotel behind the tour as one unit.

June through August, room rates are highest, and reservations are imperative, as local tourists arrive in droves to visit the bay. Costs can be higher on weekends for the same reason.

VND210,000-525,000
The bright, spotless rooms at ★ Viet Hoa Hotel (35 Vuon Dao, tel. 03/3384-6035, VND210,000-315,000) are part of a string of budget hotels along Vuon Dao, but this one stands out due to its owners, who go out of their way to be helpful and are one of the only tour providers on the block that do not overcharge travelers to an alarming rate. Hot water, air-conditioning, television, Wi-Fi, and a minibar are included in the hotel's amenities, along with private balconies for street-facing rooms. Mattresses at Viet Hoa—and, indeed, most accommodations in this vicinity—are not exactly plush, so don't bother if you can't handle a solid bed.

In possession of the most impeccably clean bathrooms in Ha Long City, New Century Hotel (The Ky Moi) (27 Vuon Dao, tel.

Ha Long City

Tuan Chau Island

TUAN CHAU

TUAN CHAU PIER

FERRY TO/FROM CAT BA ISLAND

HOANG QUOC VIET

18

BAI CHAY BUS STATION

VIETCOMBANK

NOVOTEL

LY QUOC SUR

BAI CHAY

HA LONG

LINH DAN

GRAND HA LONG HOTEL

VINACE

BAMBOO BAR

TOURIST INFORMATION CENTER

HONG HANH 3

BAI CHAY BEACH

EMERAUDE CAFÉ

THONG NHAT 2

HA LONG EDEN

POST OFFICE

NEW CENTURY HOTEL

VIET HOA

BAI CHAY PIER

BMC-HAI AU

SEE DETAIL

HA LONG

HA LONG

CAU LY BAI CHAY

Ha Long Bay

Chu Luc Bay

HON GAI BUS STATION

HON GAI PIER

QUANG NINH GENERAL HOSPITAL

Vung Oan Island

Hang Ma Island

Hang Dinh Island

Gieng Goi Island

Do Island

Met Island

0 25 km

0 25 mi

© AVALON TRAVEL

Seeing the Bay in One Day

It's possible to access some of Ha Long's more popular sights in a single day. Four-, six-, and eight-hour cruises are available through Ha Long City's hotels and the city's ticketing office at Bai Chay Pier. These tours stop at Dau Go and Thien Cung Caves, a floating fishing village, Titov Island, and Sung Sot Cave, depending upon the length of the outing. The six- and eight-hour excursions are a pleasant way to pass a day.

For the most inexpensive tours, public boats at Bai Chay Pier (Ha Long, tel. 03/3384-6592, www.benxebentauquangninh.vn, 6:30am-4:30pm daily, VND100,000 pp) cast off every day at 8am, visiting Thien Cung and Dau Go Caves as well as a few of the bay's more famous landmarks. Factor in additional costs for the bay's entry fee (VND120,000) as well as VND50,000 for each of the sights visited. Bai Chay only offers four-hour excursions.

For longer trips, private boats can also be hired at the pier. With costs beginning at VND400,000-500,000 per hour, you may prefer to arrange through a hotel or booking agency, where you can find six- and eight-hour excursions that tack on activities like swimming and kayaking as well as a few more of the bay's sights.

The hotel or booking agent will almost certainly charge a commission, though the amount can vary drastically depending upon the company. A six-hour tour of the bay, including lunch and all entry fees, should come to around VND600,000 per person. Some agencies will quote VND1,000,000 or more. Ask for a breakdown of the included costs so that you can see just how much goes to the hotel or booking agency. Day tours from high-end cruise providers begin around VND1,000,000, so booking at or above this price through a local hotel or booking agency is probably not worth your money. To avoid some of this hassle, pay a visit to the folks at Viet Hoa Hotel (35 Vuon Dao, tel. 03/3384-6035), who are a trustworthy group and tend to charge more reasonable prices.

Once you have booked your tour, request that the booking agent write down all included sights, activities, and amenities on your receipt. Because the booking agency and the tour operator are often different companies, miscommunications can arise. With many of the boat guides speaking limited English, a record of your itinerary can help to resolve any issues.

It is also possible to arrange a daylong outing with higher-end cruise companies, though most of these tours originate in Hanoi. This requires a four-hour drive to and from the city (from VND1,155,000). With only a fraction of the day spent on the water, it's far more worthwhile to organize an overnight excursion if you plan to enter this price range.

03/3384-4314, VND252,000-315,000) makes for a solid budget option. Rooms are basic but spacious and count Wi-Fi access, a television, hot water, air-conditioning, and a fridge in their amenities, though beds are hard. Cheap boat trips can be arranged from here, as well as motorbike rentals, transportation, and a whole host of other add-ons.

Hidden in the shadow of Muong Thanh across the street, Ha Long Eden (Ha Long, tel. 03/3384-6145, VND480,000-900,000) may not be a five-star affair, but its rooms represent good value for money. Clean, well-appointed accommodations come with comfy beds, hot water, air-conditioning, television, and Wi-Fi access. Some rooms include

pleasant views of the bay, and the staff are an amiable bunch. Prices can go up as much as 15 percent on weekends, as this is when more local tourists visit. During the off-season, this isn't an issue.

Beside Ha Long Eden, Thong Nhat 2 (Ha Long, tel. 09/1716-8999, VND400,000-900,000) is a slightly older hotel whose view is somewhat obscured by its next-door neighbor. Nonetheless, rooms are well-kept, featuring Wi-Fi access, television, air-conditioning, and hot water. Rooms at the back offer partial views of the bay. Should you find that Thong Nhat 2 is full, check out the other Thong Nhats (1, 3, and 4) on either side.

A short uphill jaunt from the main drag,

the rooms at Linh Dan (104 Bai Chay, tel. 03/3652-2696, www.linhdanhalong.com, VND300,000) are spacious and clean, featuring large windows, Wi-Fi access, television, hot water, air-conditioning, and a fridge. Bathrooms are on the small side, but the hotel's location offers more peace and quiet than some of the other accommodations closer to the bay.

OVER VND2,100,000

While it's not a four-star accommodation as advertised, the Grand Ha Long (Ha Long, tel. 03/3384-4042, www.grandhalonghotel. com.vn, VND1,900,000-5,300,000, breakfast included) is a worthy option for this price range. Rooms are well-appointed, featuring standard amenities as well as Wi-Fi access. Though the furniture is slightly undersized, beds are comfortable. Use of the swimming pool is included in the room rate. Some rooms offer a nice view of the bay overlooking Bai Chay Beach. Downstairs, the hotel operates a restaurant and bar within its retro lobby.

★ Novotel Ha Long Bay (Ha Long, tel. 03/3384-8108, www.novotelhalong.com.vn, VND3,230,000-5,220,000) is the sole standout in the high-end price range. Of the four different room types, the bay-facing rooms are best, affording incredible views and large bathtubs, cozy beds, and a balcony. Downstairs are a swanky restaurant, café, and an outdoor seating area that overlooks the bay. Spa services and a fitness center are available to guests, as are cooking classes, kayaking, city tours, and bay cruises. Breakfast can be included for a few extra dollars.

Food

The strip along Bai Chay Beach offers enough culinary variety for a day or two. The city's one specialty is its seafood, which comes from the bay and is particularly fresh.

Come dinner time, the Hong Hanh 3 (Ha Long, tel. 03/3381-2345, 6am-10pm daily, VND95,000-200,000) is often busy, doling out excellent local seafood in both its cozy interior and on the patio next door. Dishes are prepared family-style and therefore more expensive. Service is quick and the place is popular with locals, too.

A good lunch or dinner spot, the hotel restaurant at Linh Dan (104 Bai Chay, tel. 03/3384-6025, www.linhdanhalong.com, 8am-8pm daily, VND70,000-200,000) does a tasty turn in seafood, from shrimp and squid to snails and fish, as well as a handful of beef and chicken offerings. Seats are available indoors and out. The prices are right for these delicious meals.

A bright orange building opposite Bai Chay Pier, BMC - Hai Au (Ha Long, tel. 03/3384-5065, www.haiaujunk.com, 7am-10pm daily, VND20,000-150,000) is more café than restaurant with a longer list of drinks—coffee, tea, beer, wine, and cocktails—than food. Portions are generous and make for a filling breakfast or lunch.

The small, windowed dining room at Vinace (Ha Long, tel. 03/3351-1538, 8am-midnight daily, VND115,000-230,000) serves pizza, pasta, risotto, and seafood dishes that, while not exactly authentic Italian cuisine, are a delicious and worthy Western option. Its wine list and European coffee, plus desserts like tiramisu, round out the menu. Look for the bright red "Italian" sign flashing just opposite Emeraude Cafe.

Among the many boxy buildings lining the road behind Bai Chay Beach, Bamboo Bar (Ha Long, tel. 03/3364-0899, baranhphong@vnn.vn, 7am-2am daily, VND50,000-150,000) is a cheerful spot outfitted in bamboo and offering burgers, pasta, pizza, and a few Vietnamese options, as well as beer, wine, and cocktails. Western food prices are more reasonable than other nearby restaurants and the staff are a friendly bunch.

One of the swankier outlets on the strip, Emeraude Cafe (Ha Long, tel. 03/3384-9266, www.emeraude-cruises.com, 8am-9pm daily, VND80,000-355,000) does a reasonable take on Western food like burgers, steak, and pizza, though portions run small. European coffee is available. The servers are attentive and friendly. The building, a pretty white bungalow with arched windows, features wireless Internet and a bank of computers for customer use, as well as plenty of magazines and newspapers to while away the hours.

Information and Services
TOURIST INFORMATION
Ha Long's local **tourist information center** (Ha Long, tel. 03/3362-8862, www.halongtourism.com.vn, 8:30am-5pm daily) does a great job of cluing travelers in on all of the sights both in the bay and beyond, provided you ask the right questions. Look to the giant wall map inside the office for a bit of guidance and feel free to inquire about the office's complimentary info booklet, a small paperback printed by the bay's management department that details the history of the area as well as giving a round-up of its most famous attractions. Maps of the bay are available free of charge.

Ha Long is one of the few cities in Vietnam that has an active **tourist hotline** (tel. 03/3384-7347). While there's no guarantee that your complaint will be addressed, any issues you might have regarding tourism in the city or the bay can be lodged here.

BANKS
ATMs are all over Ha Long road. For currency exchange, the local **Vietcombank** (Ha Long, tel. 03/3381-1808, www.vietcombank.com.vn, 7:30am-11:30am and 1pm-4:30pm Mon.-Fri.) near Bai Chay Pier can help.

INTERNET AND POSTAL SERVICES
A large **post office** (To 1, Khu 2, Ha Long, tel. 03/3384-6203, 7:30am-11:30am and 1pm-5pm Mon.-Sat., 8:30am-10:30am and 2:30pm-4pm Sun.) sits on the corner of Ha Long and Vuon Dao streets and provides mail services.

For Internet access, most hotel rooms come with Wi-Fi access. If you're in need of a computer, the **tourist information center** (Ha Long, tel. 03/3362-8862, www.halongtourism.com.vn, 8:30am-5pm daily) offers 30 minutes of free Internet use at the desktop computers in its office. You can also grab a drink at the

Emeraude Cafe (Ha Long, tel. 03/3384-9266, www.emeraude-cruises.com, 8am-9pm daily), where a bank of computers with Internet access is available to customers.

MEDICAL SERVICES
Quang Ninh General Hospital (Tue Tinh, tel. 03/3382-5489, www.benhviendktinhquangninh.vn) is the best medical facility in the area. For any serious conditions, head to Hanoi.

Getting There
BUS
From Hanoi (4 hours, VND200,000), minibuses most often drop off passengers along Vuon Dao or the main strip. The majority of budget and mid-range cruise outfitters include bus transportation from Hanoi in the cost. If you don't have a tour booked in advance, any travel agent or hotel in Hanoi can arrange a minibus to transport you to Ha Long City. This costs more than taking a local bus from Hanoi (VND80,000-100,000), but the tourist bus will pick you up from your hotel.

The **Bai Chay bus station** (near corner of Le Huu Trac and QL18, tel. 03/3364-9230) sits just over three miles from the Bai Chay Pier. From here, daily buses depart for Hanoi.

BOAT
From Gia Luan port on the northern side of Cat Ba Island, a **local ferry** (VND50,000) runs at 9am, 1pm, and 4pm every day (confirm ahead of time during the off-season). The ride across the bay takes about 1.5 hours. It lands seven miles from Bai Chay at the southern end of **Tuan Chau Island** (Tuan Chau Island, tel. 03/3655-0009, www.tuanchau-halong.com.vn).

Make the trip back from Cat Ba into Ha Long City, or book a bus-boat-bus ticket (wherein the bus boards a ferry) from Cat Ba directly to your next destination. Those who arrive in Ha Long City via Tuan Chau Island will have to either snap up one of the few *xe om* drivers loitering around the ferry dock or opt for a taxi into town. A *xe om* ride costs around VND80,000, while a cab ride is about VND130,000.

Getting Around

The *xe om* drivers of Ha Long are particularly eager to help you find your way: Expect to receive more than a few honks, shouts, and catcalls walking down the main road. For taxis, the local Mailinh (tel. 03/3362-8628) cabs are one of a few companies in town.

Many of the hotels along Vuon Dao rent out motorbikes or bicycles to travelers. Those that provide this service tend to advertise it on the front door, so you shouldn't have too much trouble finding a vehicle.

HAIPHONG

The third-largest city in Vietnam, Haiphong is a hectic northern port seldom visited by foreign travelers but for a few who use the town as a transit point en route to Cat Ba Island. Haiphong's bustling streets function as a significant economic and political center up north as well as an important transportation hub for imports and exports within the country. You will find a few traces of colonial architecture in town, leftover from the days of the French, who aided in developing Haiphong's port during the 1870s, as well as a monument to revered local and national hero Le Chan, a gutsy female general who led the charge against Chinese colonists in the third century.

Given the fact that Haiphong's major draw is its daily hydrofoils to Cat Ba Island, a stopover in the city needn't last more than one night. In the downtown area, and specifically along Dien Bien Phu, there are plenty of hotels, restaurants, and other necessities to tide you over until your boat comes. A stroll along the former Bonnal Canal or a quick visit to one of the local pagodas can keep you entertained.

Sights

There are a handful of sights around Haiphong that can be explored in an afternoon, most of them on foot. When visiting Haiphong's pagodas and temples, dress respectfully, as the local reception of foreign tourists is sometimes stony and any revealing clothes will likely not be well-received.

HAIPHONG MUSEUM

The Haiphong Museum (66 Dien Bien Phu, tel. 03/1382-3451, 8am-11am Tues., 8am-11am and 7:30pm-9:30pm Wed.-Sun., VND5,000) is a Gothic behemoth situated right in the center of town. Covering a hectare of land, the large colonial-style building was completed in 1919 and houses a nice collection of ancient ceramics and wood carvings from the Le and Tran dynasties, vintage photographs from the days of French colonialism, and a few other odds and ends, including a coin collection, an old-school Mobylette bike, and a rickshaw. The standard exhibit on Vietnamese sovereignty in the Paracel and Spratly islands is also on display. English signage is available, but translations are only sometimes comprehensible. This is not a bad spot to pass the time if you're wandering around town.

HAIPHONG PARK

A sliver of land winding from Dien Bien Phu around to the Tam Bac River, Haiphong's local park lies in the center of town and boasts a charming esplanade, complete with flower stalls and manicured gardens. Once the Bonnal Canal during colonial days, parts of this waterway have been filled in, but a small stretch remains, complementing some of Haiphong's other architectural sights, including the Opera House and a generous statue of Le Chan (intersection of Me Linh and Nguyen Duc Canh), local heroine and revered Vietnamese historical figure. The statues is over 24 feet tall and weighs 19 tons.

OPERA HOUSE

If you're strolling along the parkway downtown, chances are you'll pass Haiphong's Opera House (65 Dinh Tien Hoang, tel. 03/1382-3084), a grand, pale yellow colonial hall completed in 1904. Built by the French, this 400-seat theater is shuttered on most

Haiphong

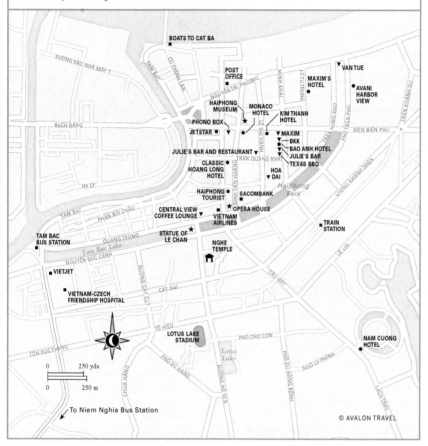

days, but its architecture complements the waterfront scene and the large open square before it.

NGHE TEMPLE

From the outside, **Nghe Temple (Den Nghe)** (sunrise-sunset daily) appears to be nothing special, its stark gray walls rubbing shoulders with a local schoolyard. But, through the three-door entrance gate is a lavish homage to local hero Le Chan, a female general who aided in the 2nd century uprising of the Trung sisters.

Born in An Bien, a small village northwest of Haiphong, Le Chan was from a well-to-do family. But, at the time, Chinese colonization meant that even the upper echelons of Vietnamese society were subject to oppression. When To Dinh, the leader of what was then known as Giao Chi, a Chinese territory, attempted to make Le Chan his wife, she refused, an act of dissent that caused To Dinh to harm her parents. For 10 years, Le Chan bided her time until, in the spring of AD 40, the Trung sisters launched a rebellion against the Chinese occupation, driving To Dinh and his army out of Vietnam. Le Chan and her forces were instrumental in this takeover. Two years later, the Chinese returned in greater numbers, rekindling the battle. The Trung sisters, who had ruled Vietnam in the interim, committed suicide rather than risk capture by the Han Chinese. Upon their death, Le Chan continued to fight for another year, falling back to fiercely defend the village of Lat Son until, in AD 43, when defeat was inevitable, she threw herself off Giat Dau mountain. Vietnam's remaining generals buried her in secret and she has been a revered hero ever since.

The original temple on this site was no more than a modest shrine. Today's two main halls, built in 1919 and renovated several times over the years, are ornate and intricate. Several stone animals, including elephants, horses, and lions, populate the courtyard, while Le Chan's altar is off to the right. Beautiful floral arrangements surround the legendary woman's statue, and lacquered woodwork hangs overhead.

Nghe Temple

Entertainment and Events
NIGHTLIFE

Nightlife in Haiphong is fairly tame, with most locals gathering for a cup of coffee after work or an evening glass of wine. All of the city's bars and cafés shut their doors by midnight.

The narrow, dimly lit **Julie's Bar** (22C Minh Khai, tel. 03/1352-1198, www.juliesbarhaiphong.vn, 5pm-last customer daily, VND20,000-120,000) gets livelier later in the evening, starting around 8pm, and a friendly staff serves beer and cocktails. A good music selection plays in the background, making this an inviting spot for a nighttime drink.

The cozy little café at **Phono Box** (79 Dien Bien Phu, tel. 03/1382-3333, 9am-midnight daily, VND25,000-160,000) makes a nice setting for a mellow evening drink, with exposed brick walls, leather chairs, and a collection of throwback records on repeat. Beer and cocktails are served alongside a lengthy wine selection, and you'll also find full Western meals (from VND90,000).

With cushy retro sofa chairs and saxophone music in the background, **Maxim** (51 Dien Bien Phu, tel. 03/1382-2934, 6:30am-11pm daily, VND20,000-90,000) gives off a laid-back jazz-lounge vibe. Though it's most popular during the evenings, this corner property in downtown Haiphong gets regular visitors throughout the day, when it functions as a café. Occasional live music and a mellow atmosphere really get things rolling after dark. Reasonably priced food (from VND40,000) is also served.

FESTIVALS AND EVENTS

Toward the start of September each year, the annual **Do Son Buffalo Fighting Festival,** a long-held tradition, takes place 12 miles south of the city center. Shortly after the Lunar New Year, local participants begin their search for a prize buffalo. Once a trainer has settled upon a chosen animal, he or she prepares the buffalo to fight. Training can last up to eight months.

The preliminary stages of the competition take place around late June or early July, with the first showdown held on the eighth day of the sixth lunar month. These contests continue up until the ninth day of the eighth lunar month (early September), when the final competition is attended by scores of Vietnamese from near and far.

During the competition, buffaloes do not harm one another; rather, the animals lock horns to assert their strength. The loser usually flees, chased by the winner, signaling the end of a fight. After the festival, all the buffaloes are slaughtered. Their blood is offered to the Jade Emperor, while the meat is sold at the market and its consumption is believed to be good luck.

Accommodations

Accommodation costs tend to be higher in Haiphong than other Vietnamese cities. The best value options run no less than VND250,000 in most places. Conditions in the city's cheaper hotels are pretty abysmal and make it worth shelling out the extra couple bucks for a comfier bed and a room that's been properly cleaned. On the more expensive end, you can find plenty of well-appointed mid-range and top-tier accommodations thanks to Haiphong's regular business visitors.

VND210,000-525,000

One of the better mid-range options, Kim Thanh Hotel (67 Dien Bien Phu, tel. 03/1374-5264, www.kimthanhhotel.com.vn, VND395,000-550,000) is clean and well kept, though its beds are of the more solid variety. TV, air-conditioning, hot water, and Wi-Fi are in each room, and the staff assists with general queries regarding Haiphong.

The well-kept ★ Maxims Hotel (3K Ly Tu Trong, tel. 03/1374-6540, www.maximshotel.vn, VND420,000-890,000) is your best bet when it comes to mid-range accommodations in Haiphong. Rooms are clean and feature modern furnishings with comfy beds, air-conditioning, TV, and Wi-Fi access. The downstairs restaurant serves food throughout the day and staff can assist with travel-related queries. Due to the limited number of mid-range options in town, this hotel is often full; check availability before arriving.

Though it's fairly basic, Bao Anh Hotel (20B Minh Khai, tel. 03/1382-3406, www. hotelbaoanh.com, VND400,000-1,000,000) boasts one of the better locations in town, alongside a street full of restaurants and close to the city center. Accommodations are clean, modern, and equipped with TV, Wi-Fi,

Maxims Hotel

a minibar, hot water, and air-conditioning. Breakfast is included in the room rate, though you're better off skipping the rather limited selection and venturing out on your own.

VND525,000-1,050,00

A clear step above the less-expensive mid-range options in Haiphong, Monaco Hotel (103 Dien Bien Phu, tel. 03/1374-6468, www.haiphongmonacohotel.com, VND600,000-800,000) boasts a spacious reception area decked out in European decor and, inexplicably, a pair of sphinxes guarding the main staircase. The staff are hit-or-miss here. Rooms are plush as far as mid-range accommodations go, featuring television, Wi-Fi access, hot water, air-conditioning, a minibar, and modern furnishings. Breakfast is included in the room rate.

VND1,050,000-2,100,00

The palatial reception hall at Classic Hoang Long Hotel (25 Tran Quang Khai, tel. 03/1328-2666, www.classic-hoanglonghotel.com, VND1,460,000-3,160,000) is chock full of mismatched decorations, from Greek statues to Buddhist figurines, a replica of an ancient Vietnamese brass drum, and a grand, wraparound staircase. While rooms upstairs don't necessarily live up to this same eclectic style, the accommodations at Classic Hoang Long are well-appointed, featuring hot water, air-conditioning, TV, Wi-Fi access, and, in the case of VIP rooms, retro furniture, tea- and coffee-making facilities, and an in-room computer. Breakfast is included in the room rate.

OVER VND2,100,00

The rather posh Nam Cuong Hotel (47 Lach Tray, tel. 03/1382-8555, www.namcuonghaiphonghotel.com.vn, VND1,800,000-3,900,000) sits a short way south of the park and boasts four varieties of high-end accommodations, all of which are outfitted with a host of amenities, including Wi-Fi access and daily, fresh fruit and water. Guests are also invited to a welcome drink and can enjoy the daily complimentary buffet breakfast in the hotel restaurant. Use of the sauna, whirlpool tub, and swimming pool are all free of charge.

Overlooking the water, AVANI Harbor View (12 Tran Phu, tel. 03/1382-7827, www.avanihotels.com, VND2,730,000-3,675,000) is Haiphong's best accommodation. An updated grand colonial-style building, complete with arched windows and balustrades, this four-star hotel houses 122 guest rooms, two restaurants, two bars, a swimming pool, spa, and fitness center. Rooms come in varying levels of luxury, but each bright and well-appointed room features television, Wi-Fi access, a minibar, tea- and coffee-making facilities, a spacious sitting area, work desk, and in-room safe. Hotel eateries serve a range of Asian and Western cuisines, and additional activities like tai chi and cooking classes are available.

Food

At Hoa Dai (39 Le Dai Hanh, tel. 03/1382-2098, 7am-11pm daily, VND40,000-80,000), the laminated page upon which the restaurant lists its menu selection is entirely in Vietnamese. Thankfully, the owner speaks a few words of English and there are some handy ClipArt illustrations to guide you. You'll find beef, pork, and fish among the offerings. Prices are not written on the menu, so ask beforehand.

Though its faded white exterior could use a renovation, the lively Van Tue (1A Hoang Dieu, tel. 03/1374-6338, www.vantue.com.vn, 9am-9pm daily, VND45,000-350,000) is a popular local restaurant that serves all manner of Vietnamese cuisine, including scores of beef, chicken, pork, and vegetarian dishes, including more adventurous fare like frog and eel. Staff speak some English and the price tag makes Van Tue not only one of the more active spots in town but also one of the more affordable.

An extension of the establishment of the same name on Minh Khai, Julie's Bar (24A Le Dai Hanh, 9am-midnight daily, VND60,000-120,000) is a cheap and cheerful Indian food joint that offers both quiet indoor seating and a pleasant upstairs patio from which to watch the street below. Its selection is limited to a few curries and one or two vegetarian dishes. The staff are friendly, and you'll find beer, cocktails, coffee, and other refreshments.

The chic and sophisticated BKK (22A Minh Khai, tel. 03/1382-3994, bkk_haiphong@hotmail.com, 10am-10pm daily, VND75,000-225,000) serves delicious Thai and pan-Asian cuisine, including coconut curries and spicy salads, in a posh colonial building just off the main drag. Its extensive wine collection, sleek wooden furniture, and collection of black-and-white vintage photographs add to the experience. Dine inside or al fresco on the equally classy front patio. Prices are more expensive but fit the style and service of the place.

Down a street of international restaurants, Texas BBQ (22H Minh Khai, tel. 03/1365-3450, www.texasbbq.com.vn, 8am-10pm daily, VND85,000-500,000) is the only spot in town to offer Tex-Mex cuisine, including quesadillas, tacos, and enchiladas, as well as pizza, burgers, and steak, making for a hearty departure from local cuisine. Delivery service is available, but the bright, narrow dining room is equally inviting.

While there are droves of small local cafés in Haiphong, Central View Coffee Lounge (Central Tower, 43 Quang Trung, 4th Fl., tel. 03/1626-0808, 7:30am-11pm daily, VND25,000-90,000) is a swankier version, perched above a few floors of offices in the downtown Central Tower, which overlooks the city's main park, offering a breezy, pleasant view of the bustle below. Both Vietnamese and European coffee is served, as well as fruit shakes, tea, and alcohol in the evenings.

Information and Services

Haiphong Tourist (65 Hoang Van Thu, tel. 03/1356-9600, www.haiphongtourism.gov.vn, 7am-11:30am and 2pm-5pm daily) has a small tourist information kiosk that can supply you with free city maps, helpful advice, and a handy guide booklet with plenty of hotel and restaurant recommendations as well as some background on the city's sights.

You should have no trouble locating an ATM downtown. The local Sacombank (119-121 Dinh Tien Hoang, tel. 03/1356-9113, www.sacombank.com.vn, 7:30am-11:30am and 1pm-4:30pm Mon.-Fri., 7:30am-11:30am Sat.) exchanges currency.

The city's central post office (3 Nguyen Tri Phuong, tel. 03/1382-3004, 7am-8pm daily) assists with all mail-related queries.

The largest and best-equipped local hospital is the Vietnam-Czech Friendship Hospital (Benh Vien Viet-Tiep) (1 Nha Thuong, tel. 03/1383-2721), though any serious illnesses or injuries should be brought to Hanoi.

Getting There
BOAT
Speedboats make daily trips to Haiphong from Cat Ba Island. Slightly tired but functional vessels are operated by Cat Ba Island Resort and Spa (4 Ben Binh, tel. 03/1358-8999, www.catbaislandresort-spa.com, VND200,000), with departures at 8am, 10am, 2pm, and 4pm. The trip takes about 45 minutes. Boats depart from the town's main pier, just opposite 1 Thang 4 street. Other speedboat options are available for the same cost, but the boats are smaller and the travel time longer.

BUS
Shuttles depart every 10 minutes daily from Hanoi's Luong Yen and Gia Lam bus stations (two hours, VND80,000) for Haiphong, arriving at Tam Bac bus station (corner of Tam Bac and Quang Trung, tel. 03/1385-8067, 4:30am-9pm daily).

From southern destinations like Ninh Binh (2.5 hours, VND160,000), buses stop at Niem Nghia bus station (Tran Nguyen Han), about two miles from the city center; the same station should be used to travel south from Haiphong.

Hoang Long (45 Le Thanh Tong, tel. 03/1355-2866, www.hoanglongasia.com,

8am-5pm daily, VND110,000) receives two daily buses from Cat Ba via the bus-boat-bus route. Buses depart from Cat Ba's town center each afternoon.

TRAIN

Though it's not wired into the general north-south Reunification Line, Haiphong's train station (75 Luong Khanh Thien, tel. 03/1392-1333, 7am-5pm daily) is connected to Hanoi. Trains from Hanoi (2.5 hours, VND60,000) make daily runs to Haiphong. Expect to pay more for soft seats.

AIR

Flying is the least popular and most expensive way of getting to Haiphong, but it's possible. Cat Bi International Airport (HPH, Le Hong Phong, tel. 03/1397-6408) sits five miles southeast of downtown Haiphong and welcomes multiple daily flights from Danang and Saigon (2 hours, VND900,000-1,500,000). Vietnam Airlines (ticketing office 166 Hoang Van Thu, Haiphong, tel. 03/1381-0890, www.vietnamairlines.com), VietJet (ticketing office 7 Tran Nguyen Han, Haiphong, tel. 03/1363-0032, www.vietjetair.com) and Jetstar (ticketing office 36 Hoang Van Thu, Haiphong, tel. 03/1355-9550, www.jetstar.com) serve Cat Bi airport and have ticketing offices in town.

Getting Around

For four-wheeled vehicles, try a local Mailinh (tel. 03/1383-3833) or Hai Phong (tel. 03/1373-7373) taxi. As usual, *xe om* are present on street corners across town.

Hired vehicles can be arranged through several hotels. As a less-touristed destination, you won't find many affordable motorbike rentals, so be prepared to jump on a *xe om* if necessary, or stick to exploring on foot. If you prefer a bicycle, most accommodations don't advertise the option but it is possible to procure a bike from some hotel receptionists.

Ninh Binh

Sixty miles south of Hanoi, the small, provincial town of Ninh Binh may not come off as a worthy tourist destination, but venture out west and you'll be greeted by the sharp and mysterious limestone peaks of Tam Coc and Trang An. Known as "Ha Long Bay on Land," Ninh Binh's serene flooded fields stand in stark contrast to its scores of karst formations, casually rising out of the pancake-flat landscape and shrouded in lush jungle greenery. Throw in a handful of ancient temples and one of the earliest capitals in Vietnamese civilization, all of which fit nicely into the romantic, mist-obscured countryside, and you've got reason enough to spend at least a day in Ninh Binh.

Several Hanoian tour companies make day trips to the area, hitting Tam Coc, Bich Dong Pagoda, and the nearby rice paddies, but it's just as easy to do the trip on your own. Given the modest costs of accommodation and food, Ninh Binh is an excellent spot from which to explore northern Vietnam's stunning scenery, especially in the cold and misty winter. Summer brings plenty of sun and better visibility. Tam Coc is best enjoyed during April and May, before the rice harvest takes away its signature paddy fields. Trang An is at its best around October, when water levels are low and the area's caves are more accessible.

Trang An and Tam Coc are a short drive or cycle away from Ninh Binh. Blue-and-white road signs are posted here and there to help direct you. Most hotels and guesthouses can either arrange a tour for you on the spot or point you in the direction of one. Most sights around Ninh Binh will require a boat,

Ninh Binh

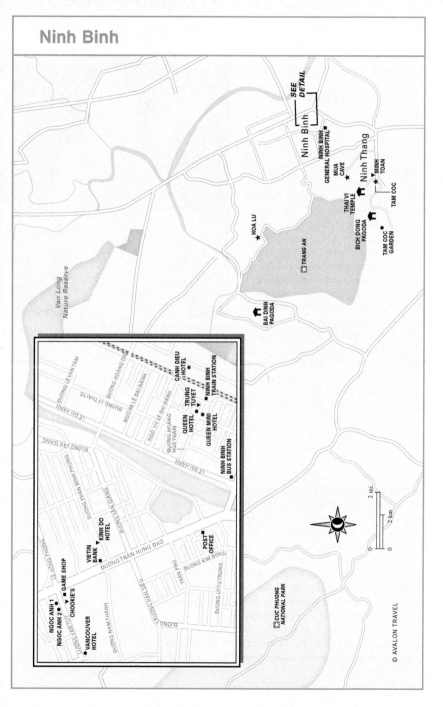

SEE DETAIL

Ninh Binh

NINH BINH GENERAL HOSPITAL

MUA CAVE

Ninh Thang

MINH TOAN

TAM COC

THAI VI TEMPLE

HOA LU

TRANG AN

BICH DONG PAGODA

TAM COC GARDEN

Van Long Nature Reserve

BAI DINH PAGODA

DUONG LE VAN TAM

DUONG HOANG DIEU

LE DAI HANH

DUONG LY THAI TO

CANH DIEU HOTEL

NGO 89 LE DAI HANH

NINH BINH TRAIN STATION

TRUNG TUYET

DUONG HOANG HOA THAM

NGO 111 LE DAI HANH

QUEEN HOTEL

QUEEN MINI HOTEL

LE DAI HANH

NINH BINH BUS STATION

DUONG PHAN DINH PHUNG

DUONG VAN GIANG

DUONG VAN GIANG

LE HONG PHONG

KINH DO HOTEL

VIETIN BANK

DUONG TRAN HUNG DAO

POST OFFICE

DUONG TRAN PHU

DUONG KIM DONG

NGOC ANH 1

NGOC ANH 2

GAME SHOP

CHOOKIE'S

DUONG LAN TUY

VANCOUVER HOTEL

DUONG NAM THANH

DUONG PHAN SET

DUONG TRUONG HAN SIEU

DUONG LY TU TRONG

CUC PHUONG NATIONAL PARK

2 mi

0

2 km

0

© AVALON TRAVEL

as the best views in the area are from the water. Rowboat rides tend to take more time than the average sight, with most trips lasting 2-3 hours, so plan your day accordingly.

TAM COC AND VICINITY
Tam Coc

Long touted as Ninh Binh's main event, Tam Coc (7am-5pm daily, VND80,000 entry, VND100,000 boat) is a meandering waterway that weaves through emerald-hued rice paddies and under great limestone karsts. In the flooded country fields, farmers have worked around the soaring mountains that interrupt Tam Coc's otherwise-flat terrain, creating an eye-catching array of greenery and rutted cliffs. Now an increasingly popular stop among travelers, some of the area's luster has been lost to concrete embankments along the canal and a healthy contingent of souvenir vendors and other touts, but the beauty of the area remains undeniable.

At the boating dock, a veritable army of rowers ferry passengers, usually no more than two to a boat, down the Ngo Dong River and back, often reclining to maneuver the oars with their feet, a trick which features in many tourist photo ops. The entire two-hour trip brings you through three tunnel-like caves beneath the mountains of Tam Coc before reaching the far end of the river journey.

This is where the magic begins to wear off: Thanks to the number of visitors, the area has become something of a tourist trap. At the turnaround point, a group of floating vendors lie in wait, eager to sell you a cold drink or some fruit. Should you refuse, they'll suggest that you buy a drink for your boat driver, though these are later sold back to the vendors at half-price, cutting both parties in on the profit. Some drivers even make a pit stop on the return trip to haul out their own cache of souvenirs for you to peruse. Tips are expected and freely requested at the end of the ride. This pressure to tip is higher than in other areas of Vietnam.

Quan Am statue at Bich Dong Pagoda

Thai Vi Temple

The humble Thai Vi Temple (sunrise-sunset daily, free) hearkens back to the 13th century, when rulers of the Tran dynasty thrice defeated Yuan-Mongol armies attempting to invade Vietnam. Within the small shrine, you'll find an effigy of Tran Thai Tong, a king who abdicated the throne to live as a monk after the Yuan-Mongol's first unsuccessful invasion in 1258, as well as Tran Quang Khai and Tran Hung Dao, Vietnam's most famous military general, who drove the invaders out of the country on two occasions. The countryside setting makes Thai Vi a nice tangent from the bustling main area of Tam Coc. The temple is about a half-mile from Tam Coc. Take a right just before the ticket booth on a small, narrow road, which leads out to Thai Vi.

Bich Dong Pagoda

A three-tiered mountainside masterpiece, Bich Dong Pagoda (sunrise-sunset daily, free) rambles up a limestone rock. From the bottom, a long, souvenir-lined walkway leads you across a small stone bridge to the pagoda's entrance, where the first shrine, Chua Ha, pays homage to the ancestors. Farther uphill, Chua Trung is a larger building, housing statues of the Buddha. Beyond the middle altar, a small cave winds around in an S shape, leading up to the final structure, Chua Thuong, where Quan Am has a shrine to herself. There is a beautiful (though small) white stone statue of the goddess looking out over the cliff. The views are pleasant from here. If you're keen to get all the way to the top, follow the path beyond the pagoda up to the very peak, where you can take in the surrounding fields in all their glory. It's a fairly easy walk up to the top with stairs (but not too many). The pagoda is one mile past Tam Coc, along the main road.

Mua Cave

While the actual Mua Cave (tel. 03/0361-8754, www.hangmuaninhbinh.com, 7am-5pm daily, VND50,000)—a small cavern at the base of a limestone karst—may not be worth your time, the view from the top of the nearby mountain earns this sight a place among Ninh Binh's other wondrous natural landscapes. Now part of a slightly gaudy, oversized tourism complex, the karsts bordering its far end are made accessible by a maze of 486 stone steps and zigzagging white battlements that give the place a medieval feel. Pause at each clearing and look back at the expanse of low-lying, water-logged rice paddies below. On a clear day, the views from the top, beside Mua Cave's Quan Am statue, are stunning. In the fog, its series of Buddhist spires and misty, jungle-clad hills paint an eerie, mysterious portrait of the area.

The front gate may be closed on weekdays and during the off-season. It is still possible to get inside if a caretaker is nearby. Follow the dirt track around the perimeter of the complex, where it dead-ends into the caretaker's house. Pay the entry fee and the caretaker will grant you access.

The cave is just under four miles from Ninh Binh. Ask for directions in Tam Coc.

TRANG AN AND VICINITY
★ Trang An

Winding through a maze of jungle-covered limestone karsts and picturesque countryside scenery, a ride in one of the modest wooden rowboats in Trang An (5am-5pm daily, VND150,000) is time well spent. Far less frequented by foreign tourists than the waters of Tam Coc, this stunning river landscape, dotted with temples devoted to local heroes and meandering tunnels that burrow beneath the area's rustic cliffs, is hugely popular with the Vietnamese. Business is booming at Trang An, helped by the addition of a larger, updated tourism complex and its status as a UNESCO World Heritage Site. It's the first World Heritage Site in Vietnam to receive dual distinctions, for natural and cultural properties.

It's hard to miss the brand-new boating docks, thanks to a massive billboard and the string of brightly colored flags swaying outside the main entrance. With a ticket, visitors can board one of the rowboats, which seat 4-6, and be on their way. Local boat operators are well versed in the 9.5-mile route, sometimes even rowing with their feet. It's impressive to see a single person navigate the labyrinthine passageways that snake beneath these limestone mountains with such ease. Keep an eye out for stalactites as you pass through each of Trang An's nine caves, as well as a host of other strange and otherworldly formations, from odd, concrete-like ridges to a glimpse or two of sparkly stone. One cave in particular houses a well, roughly 42 feet deep, whose water was once used for distilling rice wine; nowadays, you can see a tasteful display of ceramic jars meant to symbolize the process. There are three temple stops throughout the three-hour ride, each featuring a shrine to a different local hero connected to Ninh Binh's ancient history. It's best to arrive early in the morning to avoid the crowds, and steer clear on weekends, as Hanoians sometimes make day trips down to Ninh Binh, further adding to the madness. While you may be spared the request for a tip, it's possible that your boat driver will insist upon gratuity. You are not obligated to provide one; tip only where you feel inclined to do so.

If you're pressed for time or on a budget, you can also swing by the smaller version (6:30am-5:30pm daily, VND45,000) of Trang An farther down the road en route to Hoa Lu. This ride isn't as impressive and only lasts two hours. It's also referred to as Trang An, but the difference between the two complexes is obvious from their size.

TRINH TEMPLE

The first stop along the Trang An route, Trinh Temple is dedicated to two of King Dinh Tien Hoang's generals, Ta Thanh Tru and Huu Thanh Tru, who are credited with rescuing the king's youngest son, Dinh Toan. After the king and his two older sons were assassinated, the two generals carried the young boy into hiding. Boats stop here for 15-20 minutes to give tourists time to look around.

TRAN TEMPLE

Up and over a high limestone karst, Tran Temple lies at the end of a rambling stone staircase that reaches the peak of the mountain. The temple is a small stone structure with dragons carved into the roof. Hemmed in by thick foliage, it offers little in the way of scenic vistas. Follow the stairs down the other side of the mountain and you'll discover a modest shrine to Quy Minh Dai Vuong, a general of the 18th King Hung, the last in a line of rulers who are believed to be the founding fathers of the Vietnamese people.

The original temple was constructed during the 10th century under Dinh Tien Hoang. It was rebuilt in 1258 by emperor Tran Thai Tong, who came to Trang An and lived as a monk for a time. The altar out front is from the days of the Nguyen dynasty and is often busy with locals paying their respects. Boats stop at a dock on the far side of a karst from the temple; from there, a steep walk (about 10 minutes each way) is required to see the temple. It's possible to go inside the temple,

but the more decorative aspects are seen from the outside.

PHU KHONG

The largest of the temple areas at Trang An, Phu Khong has a few low stone buildings, decorated with yin yang tiles and dragon carvings. The most important structure is a shrine that houses eight figures. These represent a group of mandarins loyal to King Dinh Tien Hoang who, upon the assassination of their beloved leader, committed suicide in order to follow the emperor into the afterlife. Near the mandarins' temple is a Buddhist pagoda, built in the same style as its neighbors. Boats stop at Phu Khong to give visitors time to explore.

Hoa Lu

For the latter half of the 10th century, the ancient citadel at Hoa Lu (6am-6pm daily summer, 6:30am-6:30pm daily winter, VND10,000) served as the political, cultural, and economic center of the Dai Co Viet, predecessors to modern-day Vietnamese. A pair of 17th-century temples in honor of the Dinh and Tien Le dynasties stand on the grounds of the former city.

Hoa Lu was originally founded in 968 by King Dinh Tien Hoang, who was later assassinated alongside two of his sons. Le Hoan, a high-ranking military official, ascended the throne to become Le Dai Hanh, first ruler of the Tien Le dynasty.

Today, the remaining Dinh and Le temples are almost identical, with large wooden effigies of each emperor in his respective building. Dinh Tien Hoang is flanked by the two sons who died with him and his temple faces Ma Yen, the mountain atop which he was buried. In Le Dai Hanh's domain, his son sits to his right, while a memorial for his wife stands at his left. Both structures feature traditional Vietnamese architecture, including an entrance partitioned into three doors and high door frames, which force visitors to look down when entering the temple, thus showing respect to the deities inside. A stop at the Dinh and Le temples is really only worthwhile if combined with a visit to Trang An. Hoa Lu is seven miles from downtown Ninh Binh and about two miles north of the main gate at Trang An. If you're already visiting Trang An, continue on the main road to find the main entrance of Hoa Lu.

Bai Dinh Pagoda
The largest Buddhist complex in the country, Bai Dinh Pagoda (5am-5pm daily) began construction in 2004, and was completed in 2015. This massive center of worship has set several records, including the longest pagoda corridors in Asia, which trail on for over a mile from the entrance all the way up to the main hall. At the far end of a long stone bridge, a three-door front gate ushers visitors inside, where two towering guardians supervise the comings and goings at the pagoda. From here, Bai Dinh's endless covered walkways begin, rambling up the hillside accompanied by a collection of 500 stone arhat statues, each weighing five tons and standing over eight feet tall.

While there are several shrines dedicated to different statues of the Buddha and other prominent Buddhist figures, such as Quan Am, the centerpiece of this opus is the grand main hall, where a trio of enormous 50-ton, floor-to-ceiling gold-plated Buddhas sit in a row, representing the past, present, and future. Surrounded by 2,000 smaller sparkling Amitabha Buddhas set in alcoves in the walls, the sheer size of the room and its contents are enough to inspire awe in visitors. A wander around to the rest of the shrines, including a larger-than-life thousand-arms-and-eyes sculpture of Quan Am, confirm that the rest of the sprawling complex is, indeed, just as lavish.

While Bai Dinh's volume does make for an interesting spectacle, the newness of the complex detracts from its wow factor. Visitors to the pagoda usually pull up to an electric car station (VND30,000 per person one-way) just over a mile from the main entrance. You're free to walk in on your own, though it's easier to just take the ride, as you'll be doing plenty of walking once you reach the pagoda grounds.

TOWARD CUC PHUONG NATIONAL PARK
Van Long Nature Reserve
About 20 miles northwest of Ninh Binh, the Van Long Nature Reserve (Gia Van, tel. 03/0386-8798, 7am-5pm daily, VND75,000)

pond at the colossal Bai Dinh Pagoda

is a protected wetland home to hundreds of plant and animal species, including 72 varieties of birds and the largest wild population of Delacour's langurs, one of the most endangered primate species in the world. Limestone karsts dot the marsh, which is only accessible by rowboat.

If possible, it's best to time your visit during the summer, as this is when your chances of seeing wildlife are highest. Your driver will likely request a tip at the end; provide a tip at your discretion. At least half of the entrance fee goes to the nature reserve, so without a tip, the boat drivers take home only about VND35,000 for 2-3 hours' work.

TOURS

Single-day tours to Ninh Binh's main attractions can be arranged either from Ninh Binh or from Hanoi. Tours leaving from Ninh Binh tend to be more motorbike taxi services than guided excursions. While there are a few travel outfits based in the town, your best option when booking a tour in Ninh Binh is to talk to your hotel. Most accommodations can arrange a trip that includes Tam Coc, Bich Dong Pagoda, and a few other surrounding sights, though you can also pick and choose your own itinerary. You'll find a lot more variety and service in the day trips offered from Hanoi, but these excursions are more expensive, as they require transportation to and from town.

Hanoi Exposed Tours (tel. 09/4834-6026, www.hanoiexposedtours.com, VND735,000-1,785,000), the company behind local outfit Chookie's, runs tours to Tam Coc, Hoa Lu, and Bai Dinh. Asiana Travel Mate (7 Dinh Tien Hoang, tel. 04/3926-3366, www.ticvietnam.com, 8am-9pm daily) does day trips to Tam Coc.

ACCOMMODATIONS

Ninh Binh doesn't yet have droves of quality accommodations, but there are a few well-priced guesthouses and smaller, family-run hotels that do the trick. These are fairly spread out over the city's modest downtown area.

Some of the budget options surround the local train station. You can also find a string of hotels and guesthouses outside of town around the Tam Coc boat station: the upside to this location is its easy access to nearby sights. But, with Tam Coc well on the tourist trail, it's also a little exhausting to stick around here for any longer than a few minutes, as vendors and restaurant owners are quick with sales pitches.

Under VND210,000

Queen Mini Hotel (21 Hoang Hoa Tham, tel. 03/0387-1874, VND63,000 dorm, VND126,000-315,000 double) sits on a cozy corner opposite the larger Queen Hotel and not far from another similarly named accommodation. This is the most affordable of the lot and provides budget backpackers with unbelievably cheap dorm beds or private rooms that come with air-conditioning and hot showers. The staff are amiable, though expect a hard sell on things like bus tickets, vehicle rentals, and tours. Tour information is readily available and there are a handful of affordable eateries in the area.

VND210,000-525,000

Ngoc Anh Hotel (36 Luong Van Tuy, tel. 03/0388-3768, www.ngocanh-hotel.com, VND315,000-483,000, breakfast included) takes the prize for best-kept rooms in the city, with spotless tile bathrooms, comfy beds, and all the usual amenities. Three different types of rooms are available. The cheapest options run small but are perfectly adequate, while the middle- and top-tier choices are virtually the same, though the more expensive rooms come with more light. The staff is cheerful, informative, and will set you up with vehicle rentals and affordable tours of the area. You can also check out Ngoc Anh 2 (26 Luong Van Tuy, tel. 03/0388-3768, www.ngocanh-hotel.com, VND315,000-483,000), just down the road if you find that the original is full.

Canh Dieu Hotel (74 Nguyen Van Cu, tel. 03/0388-8278, www.canhdieuhotel.com.vn, VND350,000-450,000) is one of the nicer budget accommodations near the train station, with both standard and slightly larger superior rooms on offer. Hot water, air-conditioning, TV, and Wi-Fi access are all provided, along with complimentary breakfast. Additional services like laundry, tour bookings, and transportation are available.

The smartest accommodation on the block, Queen Hotel (20 Hoang Hoa Tham, tel. 03/0389-3000, www.queenhotel.vn, VND420,000-630,000) is well furnished and clean, with generous beds and enormous bathrooms. All rooms feature hot water, air-conditioning, TV, and Wi-Fi access, as well as a minibar and complimentary breakfast included in the rate. Three types of accommodations are available, from good value standard rooms to spacious deluxe beds, which also come with a balcony and bathtub. Downstairs, the hotel arranges tours and transportation to nearby sights.

VND525,000-1,050,00

The charming, family-run Vancouver Hotel (1/75 Luong Van Tuy, tel. 03/0389-3270, www.thevancouverhotel.com, VND735,000-1,365,000) sits down a quiet alley just off Luong Van Tuy and provides a rare mid-range option among mostly budget guesthouses. Its chic rooms feature Wi-Fi, television, an in-room safe, tea- and coffee-making facilities, hot water, air-conditioning, and some heavenly mattresses, alongside more space and ambience than you'll find in most of Ninh Binh's other accommodations. Breakfast is included in the room rate.

Over VND2,100,000

A tranquil boutique resort set amid rice fields, Tam Coc Garden (Hai Nham Hamlet, tel. 03/0324-9118, www.tamcocgarden.com, VND2,205,000-2,940,000) consists of 16 rustic countryside rooms. The retreat is close enough to Tam Coc to provide easy access to nearby sights, while maintaining some distance from the tourist melee. Each room offers minimalist decor and modern amenities, with plush low beds, handcrafted wooden furniture, and the famous pottery of Bat Trang

village. Wi-fi is not provided in all rooms. The bamboo-outfitted restaurant offers pleasant views of the surrounding rice paddies. Bicycle rentals are free. The friendly staff can offer local recommendations.

FOOD

Don't expect to find much variety in Ninh Binh, as most eateries remain humble, front-of-the-house set-ups with a few plastic chairs and a selection of Vietnamese dishes. The town itself is known for its goat meat, which is often served in a hotpot or with *com cháy*, another local specialty made from rice that is sun-dried and later fried. This is usually served in the same way as steamed rice, with an accompanying meat or tofu dish. Vegetarians take care, as the name of the dish can be misleading: You'll see signs all over town for *com cháy*, the Ninh Binh specialty. Vegetarian food, or *com chay,* is spelled almost exactly the same.

One of a few modest, open-front shops clustered around the train station, Trung Tuyet (14 Hoang Hoa Tham, tel. 03/0387-4510, 7am-10pm daily, VND30,000-140,000) seems to be the friendliest and best-equipped of the bunch, with welcoming owners and a host of good, cheap meals. Standard Vietnamese meals and a few backpacker favorites, including banana pancakes, appear on the menu. It's also possible to order your food in different portion sizes, depending upon your level of hunger, and you'll likely get an orange slice or two at the end of the meal as a goodwill offering.

The covered courtyard of the Kinh Do Hotel (18 Phan Dinh Phung, tel. 03/0389-9152, kinhdonb@yahoo.com, 6am-11pm daily, VND20,000-120,000) doubles as a café and restaurant during the day, serving a neat selection of Vietnamese fare, including beef, pork, chicken, and tofu dishes, as well as the local specialty, goat. Breakfast is available, and the attached hotel and tour outfit can be of use if you have travel questions.

A brand-new business near the bank of hotels on Luong Van Tuy, Chookie's (17 Luong

Van Tuy, tel. 09/4834-6026, 11am-10pm daily, VND50,000-100,000) serves as both a restaurant and the local headquarters of Hanoi Exposed Tours (hanoiexposedtours.com). Now proudly boasting the only European coffee machine in town, this bright spot is decked out in vibrant artwork and run by a friendly, English-speaking staff, which includes the knowledgeable Van, a Ninh Binh local and tour guide. The menu includes a few Vietnamese options but also offers some of the only Western food in Ninh Binh, with items like tuna melts and burgers featured on the menu. This is a great spot to visit for sound travel advice, as the staff are well-versed in Ninh Binh's tourism attractions and more than willing to help you navigate your way around town.

Just before the Tam Coc boat station, the cheerful folks at Minh Toan Restaurant (Tam Coc, tel. 09/4844-3268, 8am-8pm daily, VND30,000-180,000) offer your usual Vietnamese fare, including pork, chicken, beef, and tofu in addition to snails, goat, and com chay. Both indoor and outdoor tables are available and the family that runs the place is a little less pushy than some of the other local restaurants along the strip. This is a worthy lunch stop for those touring the Tam Coc area.

INFORMATION AND SERVICES
Tourist Information

Hotel owners are your best bet for things like maps, restaurant recommendations, and general advice. While you're not likely to find a detailed plan of Ninh Binh anywhere, the rudimentary maps offered at most accommodations do the trick, and receptionists are willing to share their knowledge with passing travelers. For additional info, you can swing by Chookie's (17 Luong Van Tuy, tel. 09/4834-6026, 11am-10pm daily), a newly opened arm of the Hanoi-based agency, Hanoi Exposed Tours.

Banks

You'll find ATMs handy along Tran Hung Dao and near many of Ninh Binh's hotels. The local Vietin Bank (951 Tran Hung Dao, tel. 03/0387-2614, www.vietinbank.vn, 7:30am-11:30am and 1:30pm-5pm Mon.-Fri., 7:30am-11am Sat.) can assist with currency exchange and has an ATM out front.

Internet and Postal Services

The central post office (1 Tran Hung Dao, tel. 03/0387-1104, 7:30am-11:30am and 1pm-6pm Mon.-Sat., 7:30am-11:30am and 1:30pm-5pm Sun.) is located near Lim Bridge. For Internet, try the game shop (1 Luong Van Tuy, 6am-11pm daily, VND4,000/hour) near Chookie's just off the main road.

Medical Services

The colossal Ninh Binh General Hospital (Benh Vien Da Khoa Ninh Binh) (Tue Tinh, tel. 03/0387-1030, www.benhvienninhbinh.vn) lies south of Lim Bridge and can deal with minor ailments, though don't expect to find an English-speaking doctor here.

TRANSPORTATION

Local buses to Ninh Binh come in from Hanoi (1.5 hours, VND160,000) and the surrounding area on a daily basis and arrive at the bus station (207 Le Dai Hanh, tel. 03/0387-1069) just opposite Lim Bridge.

The Ninh Binh train station (Hoang Hoa Tham, tel. 03/0367-3619, 7am-5pm daily) has daily runs north and south, with regular arrivals from Hanoi (2.5 hours, VND80,000 and up) and a slew of southern destinations.

Xe om can be found outside of bus stations and on street corners around town. For larger vehicles, try Mailinh (tel. 03/0363-6363) or Hoa Lu (tel. 03/0388-7888) taxis.

Most hotels and guesthouses in Ninh Binh rent out motorbikes (from VND100,000 a day) and bicycles (around VND30,000). Around the backpacker enclave at Tam Coc, prices go up, sometimes as much as double.

★ CUC PHUONG NATIONAL PARK

The oldest national park in Vietnam, Cuc Phuong National Park (Vuon Quoc Gia Cuc Phuong) (tel. 03/0384-8006, www.cucphuongtourism.com, 7am-5pm daily, VND40,000) has been protected land since 1962. It's home to several species of langurs, a fast-disappearing monkey found throughout the Asian continent. Its most famous resident, the black-and-white Delacour's langur, is among the most critically endangered primates in the world, with an estimated 200 remaining in Vietnam. Thanks to the park's conservation efforts, at least some of their diminishing numbers are protected, as are a host of other primates and turtles. Beyond these creatures, the 22,200-hectare park is also home to 336 species of birds, 76 species of reptiles, and a host of other insects, amphibians, and fish.

Cuc Phuong offers many do-it-yourself hikes throughout the park. Visit a prehistoric cave dwelling or trek through the dense jungle to see a great, towering thousand-year-old tree. Local guides can bring you on bird-watching and wildlife-spotting tours, organize homestays with the park's minority Muong population, or arrange a camping excursion in the woods. While nature hikes can be a fun way to pass the day at any time of year, Cuc Phuong is at its best March-June, when the rain recedes and more of the park's animals are out and about. Cuc Phuong is an easy and accessible trip from either Ninh Binh or Hanoi, as either a daylong or overnight excursion.

Sights

Most day visitors to Cuc Phuong get away with hitting the major highlights of the park on their own. Just before the main entrance, the visitors center provides useful maps and information. For daylong explorations of Cuc Phuong, bicycle rentals (VND100,000) make for a fun and active way to explore the park and get around to its major attractions. Visitors to the primate and turtle conservation centers are required to hire a guide (VND50,000) to introduce the animals within each complex; while it's a little unnecessary, these people manage to provide interesting information on the various endangered species within each center. Farther along, it's possible to make an independent visit to Mac Lake, a pretty little spot just inside the entrance gate, as well as the prehistoric cave and ancient tree. Park guides can be hired for lengthier

monkeys at Cuc Phuong's Endangered Primate Rescue Center

excursions into Cuc Phuong's grounds, including a trek into the jungle in search of ancient fossils, a stroll around the botanical garden, and a multi-day camping trip through the best of Cuc Phuong's foliage. All of these things can be arranged at the park's headquarters upon arrival.

Bring insect repellent, as Cuc Phuong's smallest residents can be pesky in the thick of the jungle, and substantial footwear is advised, particularly during rainy times, as the park's limestone rocks can become pretty treacherous when wet.

ENDANGERED PRIMATE RESCUE CENTER

Founded in 1993 by the Frankfurt Zoological Society, Cuc Phuong's Endangered Primate Rescue Center (9:30am-11:30am and 1:30pm-4pm daily, guide required, no separate admission) rehabilitates primates that were once a part of the illegal wildlife trade, a black-market industry fueled by demand for traditional Chinese remedies, many of which contain animal parts. Specializing in endemic species like Cuc Phuong's signature Delacour's langur and the nearby Cat Ba langur, both of which are among the most endangered primates in the world, this center cares for and studies newly rescued creatures before releasing the rehabilitated animals into a seven-hectare, semi-wild enclosure. From there, the monkeys learn to fend for themselves in the wild again before returning to their natural environment. Visitors to the center are given a tour of the animals and a brief introduction into its rescue operation. Guides take visitors to the animals' cages, where some of the more curious monkeys will approach for a closer look.

After you've paid your park entry fee at the visitors center, your guide will escort you to the rescue center.

TURTLE CONSERVATION CENTER

The Turtle Conservation Center (8am-11:30am and 1:30pm-4:30pm daily, guide required) sits opposite the Endangered Primate Rescue Center and focuses on rescuing and protecting turtles from the illegal wildlife trade, in which these creatures are used for food or traditional medicine. Visitors are able to roam the grounds, where a host of different species live in small ponds and wooded areas. An informative display explains some of the challenges and problems that stem from this ever-growing illicit industry as well as the work of the center. The turtles wander the center freely, with only low barriers separating their living spaces from the center's footpaths. Visitors are required to have guides, to protect the safety of the animals. Guides can talk more in depth about the different species.

PREHISTORIC CAVE

Discovered in 1966, the Prehistoric Cave (Dong Nguoi Xua) at Cuc Phuong National Park is believed to date back as far as 7,500 years ago. When it was first unearthed, locals came across stone implements and other ancient tools inside the cave, as well as a few tombs, suggesting that its residents were not simply cave dwellers but also practiced their own customs and traditions.

From the road, rent a flashlight (VND10,000) or bring your own to explore the darkened recesses of the cavern. It's a 300-meter walk from the road up a few flights of stone steps to the entrance, where the wide, round space is filled with miniature shrines and small incense urns. This is a nice pit stop on the way to the thousand-year-old tree and the larger Palace Cave.

The cave is about three or four miles along the park road. There will be a sign and a parking guard present on the roadside, making the cave easy to find.

PALACE CAVE AND THE THOUSAND-YEAR-OLD TREE

From the park's interior outpost (different from the office at the park entrance), it's about 30 minutes on the paved walkway to Palace Cave. Hemmed in by dense jungle on either side, this path winds through lush, canopied grounds where you may be able to spot a few creatures en route. Palace Cave is a long tunnel that's virtually untouched (so bring a flashlight).

After exploring the cave, continue on the path for about 10 minutes to the park's **thousand-year-old tree.** While this sight doesn't warrant the trip on its own, the cave is impressive and the moderate one-mile stroll through the jungle is a pleasant excursion. To make things more interesting, you can complete the full loop from the park's outpost along the paved trail to the ancient tree and then back around the long way, following a 4.3-mile dirt track back to the outpost, though be aware that this is a more challenging route. The path on this side of the loop is not maintained and is harder to follow.

Tours

Independent day tours from both Ninh Binh and Hanoi are available. Your best option is to hire a park-authorized guide, who will be able to lead you on anything from a daylong hike to a longer overnight excursion. For multiday trips, get in touch with the park beforehand, either via phone or email, to confirm a guide's availability. Cuc Phuong's website (www.cucphuongtourism.com) is a useful resource in planning your visit.

Accommodations

Cuc Phuong National Park runs a barebones **guesthouse** (VND105,000/person, VND420,000/double) with two different room options. The cheaper accommodations include an outdoor bathroom and shower but lack most basic amenities, such as hot water and air-conditioning. For a few extra dollars, you can have a standard double with indoor bathroom, as well as hot water and air-conditioning. Neither option is particularly posh, but they do the job for a short stay.

To book a room at the guesthouse, get in touch with the park's tourism office (tel. 03/0384-8006, www.cucphuongtourism. com). Availability depends upon the day. Vietnamese tourists travel in large groups, so if a Vietnamese group comes through,

the guesthouse could easily fill up in one go. Otherwise, you shouldn't have a problem arranging a room at the guesthouse, but book ahead.

Food

There are two **restaurants** (7am-8pm daily, VND20,000-150,000) within the park, one at the main headquarters and another at the park's outpost near Palace Cave and the thousand-year-old tree. The menu features plenty of grilled meats and Vietnamese dishes, as well as a limited number of vegetarian choices, at reasonable prices. There is also a snack shop just outside the visitors center.

Transportation

Cuc Phuong National Park lies roughly 35 miles from Ninh Binh and 80 miles from Hanoi. Both single- and multi-day trips to the park can be arranged from either destination.

FROM NINH BINH

Travelers departing from Ninh Binh will have to arrange transportation to the park, either by hired car, taxi, or hired motorbike. While cars run on the expensive side, particularly for individual travelers, this is a good option for groups. Make your return arrangement with the same driver, as there are no cars to hire in the park area.

Travelers who feel comfortable at the helm of a motorbike can navigate the back roads of Ninh Binh on their own, though signage is limited and English speakers are nonexistent. Depending on the weather, roads leading out to the park can become treacherous, as certain sections are more dirt track than paved highway.

From Ninh Binh, head south along 30 Thang 6 street, which turns into Highway 1 as you exit the city. The road will curve west and change names to Quang Trung. Turn right onto Dong Giao street and keep straight. It will take 24 miles to reach Cuc Phuong. Jot down the name of the national park in case you need directions. Most locals will know the park and can point you in the right direction.

FROM HANOI

From Hanoi, the same hired vehicle options apply, though travelers hoping to make the trek solo are far better to depart from Ninh Binh, as an 80-mile journey on a motorbike will eat up more of your day than the actual visit. Instead, you're better off taking the Cuc Phuong bus (VND150,000) from Hanoi's Giap Bat station at 9am and catching the return vehicle back from the park at 3pm to save yourself time and hassle. It may be wise to overnight here if you opt for the bus, as the three-hour drive leaves you little time to enjoy the park in a single day.

VEHICLES FOR HIRE

Bicycles (VND100,000/day) can be rented from Cuc Phuong's visitors center by the day to explore the park grounds.

MAP SYMBOLS

▤▤▤ Expressway	○ City/Town	✈ Airport	⚲ Golf Course
▭▭▭ Primary Road	◉ State Capital	✗ Airfield	℗ Parking Area
▭▭▭ Secondary Road	⊛ National Capital	▲ Mountain	▲ Archaeological Site
· · · · Unpaved Road	★ Point of Interest	✦ Unique Natural Feature	⛪ Church
▬▬▬ Feature Trail	• Accommodation		
- - - - Other Trail	▾ Restaurant/Bar	⬱ Waterfall	⛽ Gas Station
· · · · · · · Ferry	■ Other Location	▲ Park	ꙮ Glacier
▤▤▤ Pedestrian Walkway	Δ Campground	❏ Trailhead	▨ Mangrove
▥▥▥ Stairs		✶ Skiing Area	▨ Reef
			▨ Swamp

CONVERSION TABLES

°C = (°F – 32) / 1.8
°F = (°C x 1.8) + 32
1 inch = 2.54 centimeters (cm)
1 foot = 0.304 meters (m)
1 yard = 0.914 meters
1 mile = 1.6093 kilometers (km)
1 km = 0.6214 miles
1 fathom = 1.8288 m
1 chain = 20.1168 m
1 furlong = 201.168 m
1 acre = 0.4047 hectares
1 sq km = 100 hectares
1 sq mile = 2.59 square km
1 ounce = 28.35 grams
1 pound = 0.4536 kilograms
1 short ton = 0.90718 metric ton
1 short ton = 2,000 pounds
1 long ton = 1.016 metric tons
1 long ton = 2,240 pounds
1 metric ton = 1,000 kilograms
1 quart = 0.94635 liters
1 US gallon = 3.7854 liters
1 Imperial gallon = 4.5459 liters
1 nautical mile = 1.852 km

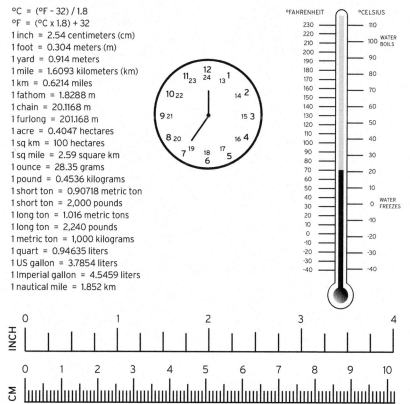

Also Available

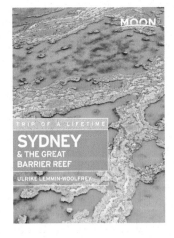

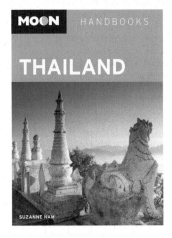

MOON SPOTLIGHT HANOI
Avalon Travel
a member of the Perseus Books Group
1700 Fourth Street
Berkeley, CA 94710, USA
www.moon.com

Editor: Leah Gordon
Series Manager: Kathryn Ettinger
Copy Editor: Naomi Adler-Dancis
Graphics Coordinators: Domini Dragoone
  and Rue Flaherty
Production Coordinator: Rue Flaherty
Cover Designer: Faceout Studios, Charles Brock
Moon Logo: Tim McGrath
Map Editor: Albert Angulo
Cartographers: Albert Angulo, Stephanie Poulain,
  Brian Shotwell

ISBN-13: 978-1-61238-920-2

Front cover photo: Evening in Hanoi's Old Quarter
© Wallaceweeks | Dreamstime.com

Title page photo © Dana Filek-Gibson

Printed in the United States of America

All recommendations, including those for sights,
activities, hotels, restaurants, and shops, are based
on each author's individual judgment. We do not
accept payment for inclusion in our travel guides,
and our authors don't accept free goods or services
in exchange for positive coverage.

Although every effort was made to ensure that
the information was correct at the time of going
to press, the author and publisher do not assume
and hereby disclaim any liability to any party for any
loss or damage caused by errors, omissions, or any
potential travel disruption due to labor or financial
difficulty, whether such errors or omissions result
from negligence, accident, or any other cause.

ABOUT THE AUTHOR

Dana Filek-Gibson

Fresh out of Emerson College, Dana Filek-Gibson moved to Vietnam as an English teacher in 2010 and never left. Though she only intended to stay for a year, Vietnam's phenomenal street food and breakneck pace hooked her from the very beginning. Over the next few months, she learned to speak Vietnamese and drive a motorbike.

Since landing a job with *AsiaLIFE*, a local magazine, Dana has written about Vietnamese culture and tourism as well as the daily adventures that come with being a redheaded expat. In 2012, she cycled from Hanoi to Ho Chi Minh City. Her wanderlust has taken her beyond Vietnam to other corners of Southeast Asia, as well as Europe, Latin America, and Africa. She is an avid runner and hopes to one day complete a marathon in Southeast Asia.

Whether ringing in the Lunar New Year like a local or learning the finer details of how to judge a chicken beauty contest, Dana counts every day in Vietnam as a new adventure.

About Moon

Moon travel guidebooks are published by Avalon Travel, a member of the Perseus Books Group. Moon was founded by Bill Dalton in 1973 with the publication of his own legendary *Indonesia Handbook*, soon followed by Handbooks to Japan, the South Pacific, and Arizona. Today, Moon specializes in guides to the United States, while also publishing books on Canada, Mexico, the Caribbean, Latin America, Europe, Asia, and the Pacific. The Avalon Travel office is in Berkeley, California, and our authors call places all over the world home.

CPSIA information can be obtained
at www.ICGtesting.com
Printed in the USA
LVOW01s1531150116

470814LV00004B/11/P